THE ULTIMATE
WOK & STIR-FRY
COOKBOOK

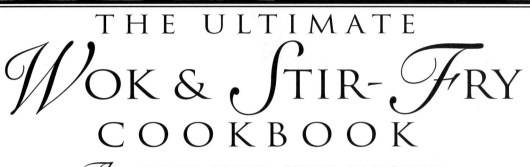

THE ULTIMATE
Wok & Stir-Fry
COOKBOOK

The BEST-EVER STEP-BY-STEP
COLLECTION
of WOK *and* STIR-FRY RECIPES
for FAST, TASTY *and* HEALTHY MEALS

CONSULTANT EDITOR : LINDA DOESER

HH
HERMES
HOUSE

This edition published in 1998 by Hermes House
27 West 20th Street, New York, NY 10011

HERMES HOUSE books are available for bulk purchase for sales promotion
and for premium use. For details, write or call the sales director,
Hermes House, 27 West 20th Street, New York, NY 10011;
(800) 354-9657

© Anness Publishing Limited 1997

Hermes House is an imprint of
Anness Publishing Limited

ISBN 1 901289 39 7

A CIP catalogue record for this book is available from the British Library

Publisher: Joanna Lorenz
Project Editor: Linda Doeser
Copy Editor: Hariette Lanzer
Designer: Ian Sandom

Photography: Karl Adamson, Edward Allwright, David Armstrong, Steve
Baxter, James Duncan, Michelle Garrett, Amanda Heywood, Patrick McLeavey,
Michael Michaels and Thomas Odulate
Styling: Madeleine Brehaut, Michelle Garrett, Maria Kelly, Blake Minton and
Kirsty Rawlings
Food for Photography: Carla Capalbo, Kit Chan, Elizabeth Wolf-Cohen, Joanne
Craig, Nicola Fowler, Carole Handslip, Jane Hartshorn, Shehzad Husain,
Wendy Lee, Lucy McKelvie, Annie Nichols, Jane Stevenson and Steven Wheeler
Illustrations: Madeleine David

Printed and bound in Singapore

1 3 5 7 9 10 8 6 4 2

CONTENTS

Introduction

Stir-frying is quick, easy, healthy and an ideal way of producing delicious and nutritious meals. However, there is even more to the versatile wok than this; it can be used for steaming, braising and deep-frying, too. Designed to spread heat quickly and evenly, it is truly a joy for any cook to use, and once you have acquired one, you will probably never want your saucepans and frying pans again!

Wok cooking originated in China, and similar techniques are widespread throughout Southeast Asia and India. Many traditional dishes from the cuisines of these countries have inspired the mouthwatering recipes in this book—from Indian curries to Chinese stir-fries and from spicy Thai vegetables to Indonesian rice dishes. Western cooks have been quick to recognize the ease and speed of wok cooking, so recipes that marry the best of East and West are also featured.

The book includes a basic introduction to caring for and using a wok and a guide to other useful kitchen equipment. This is followed by notes on some of the more exotic ingredients, as well as standard Asian sauces, spices and herbs. All the recipes are beautifully illustrated in color with easy-to-follow, step-by-step instructions. Hints and tips throughout the book advise on variations, best buys and ways of preparing some of the more unfamiliar ingredients.

You will be surprised by the vast range of stir-fried foods and other delicious recipes that can be cooked in a wok. You will soon find yourself adapting your own favorites to this technique.

THE WOK

There are many different varieties of wok available. All are bowl-shaped, with gently sloping sides that allow the heat to spread rapidly and evenly over the surface. One that is about 14 inches in diameter is a useful size for most families, allowing adequate room for deep-frying, steaming and braising, as well as stir-frying.

Originally always made from cast iron, woks are now manufactured in a number of different metals. Cast iron remains very popular, as it is an excellent conductor of heat and develops a patina over a period of time that makes it virtually nonstick. Carbon steel is also a good choice, but stainless steel tends to scorch. Nonstick woks are available but are not really very efficient because they cannot withstand the high heat required for wok cooking. They are also expensive.

Woks may have an ear-shaped handle made from metal or wood, a single long handle or both. Wooden handles are safer.

SEASONING THE WOK

New woks, apart from those with a nonstick lining, must be seasoned. Many need to be scrubbed first with dishwashing liquid to remove the manufacturer's protective coating of oil. Once the oil has been removed, place the wok over low heat and add about 2 tablespoons vegetable oil. Rub the oil over the entire inside surface of the wok with a pad of paper towels. Heat the wok slowly for 10 to 15 minutes, then wipe off the oil with more paper towels. The paper will become black. Repeat this process of coating, heating and wiping several times until the paper toweling is clean.

Once the wok has been seasoned, it should not be scrubbed again. After use, just wash it in hot water without using any detergent, then wipe it completely dry before storage. A wok in frequent use will not rust. However, if it does, scour off the rust and repeat the seasoning process.

WOK ACCESSORIES

There is a range of accessories available to go with woks, but they are by no means essential.

LID

This is a useful addition, particularly if you want to use the wok for steaming and braising, as well as frying. Usually made of aluminum, it is a close-fitting, dome-shaped cover. Some woks are sold already supplied with matching lids. However, any snug-fitting, dome-shaped saucepan lid is an adequate substitute.

STAND

This is used to provide a secure base for the wok when it is used for steaming, braising or deep-frying and is a particularly useful accessory. Stands are always made of metal but vary in form, and are usually either a simple open-sided frame or a solid metal ring with holes punched around the sides.

TRIVET

This is essential for steaming to support the plate above the water level. Trivets are made of wood or metal.

SCOOP

This is a long, often wooden-handled metal spatula with a wooden end used to toss ingredients during stir-frying. Any good, long-handled spoon can be used instead, although it does not have quite the same action.

Additional equipment is not essential for cooking with a wok, but utensils designed with this in mind—and tried and tested over time—can sometimes make the process easier. Wire and stainless steel skimmers, a wok scoop, a trivet and a selection of bamboo steamers in various sizes are among the most useful. Chinese cleavers are beautifully balanced cutting tools that can be used for both coarse and fine chopping. However, the range of cooking equipment found in most western kitchens can usually provide adequate substitutes for traditional Chinese tools and utensils.

WOK BRUSH

This bundle of stiff split bamboo is used for cleaning the wok. An ordinary kitchen brush is quite adequate.

OTHER EQUIPMENT

Most equipment required for cooking the recipes in this book will be found in any kitchen. Any specialized tools are generally simple and inexpensive, especially if you seek out authentic implements from Asian stores.

BAMBOO STEAMER

This fits inside the wok, where it should rest safely perched on the sloping sides. Bamboo steamers range in size from small, for dumplings and dim sum, to those large enough to hold a whole fish.

BAMBOO STRAINER
This wide, flat, metal strainer with a long bamboo handle makes lifting foods from steam or hot oil easier. A slotted metal spoon can also be used.

CHOPSTICKS
Extra-long wooden chopsticks are useful for stirring, fluffing up rice, separating noodles during cooking and turning and transferring items.

CLEAVER
No Chinese cook would be without one. This is an all-purpose cutting tool, available in various weights and sizes. It is easy to use and serves many purposes, from chopping up bones to precision cutting, such as deveining shrimp. It is a superb instrument for thinly slicing vegetables. It must be kept very sharp.

CHINESE GRATER
These are typically made of wood.

KARAHI PAN
Also called a Balti pan, this is the Indian equivalent of a wok and is used in much the same way. A new Karahi pan should be seasoned in the same way as a new wok.

MORTAR AND PESTLE
Usually made of earthenware, this is extremely useful for grinding small amounts of spices and for pounding ingredients together to make pastes.

FOOD PROCESSOR
This is a quick and easy alternative to the mortar and pestle for grinding spices. It can also be used for chopping and slicing vegetables.

COOKING TECHNIQUES

STIR-FRYING

This quick technique retains the fresh flavor, color and texture of ingredients. Its success depends upon having all that you require ready before starting to cook.

1 Heat an empty wok over high heat. This prevents food from sticking and will ensure even heat. Add the oil and swirl it around so that it coats the base and halfway up the sides of the wok. It is important that the oil is hot when the food is added, so that it will start to cook immediately.

2 Add the ingredients in the order specified in the recipe: usually aromatics first (garlic, ginger, scallions). If this is the case, do not wait for the oil to get so hot that it is almost smoking or they will burn and become bitter. Toss them in the oil for a few seconds. Next add the main ingredients that require longer cooking, such as dense vegetables or meat. Follow with the faster-cooking items. Toss the ingredients from the center of the wok to the sides using a wok scoop, long-handled spoon or wooden spatula.

DEEP-FRYING

A wok is ideal for deep-frying, as it uses far less oil than a deep-fat fryer. Make sure that it is fully secure on its stand before adding the oil and never leave the wok unattended.

1 Put the wok on a stand and half fill with oil. Heat until the required temperature registers on a thermometer. Alternatively, test it by dropping in a small piece of food; if bubbles form all over the surface of the food, the oil is ready.

2 Carefully add the food to the oil, using wooden chopsticks or tongs, and move it around to prevent it from sticking together. Use a bamboo strainer or slotted spoon to remove the food. Drain on paper towels before serving.

STEAMING

Steamed foods are cooked by gentle, moist heat that must circulate freely in order for the food to cook. Steaming is increasingly popular with health-conscious cooks, as it preserves flavor and nutrients. It is perfect for vegetables, meat, poultry and especially fish. The easiest way to steam food in a wok is by using a bamboo steamer.

USING A BAMBOO STEAMER

1 Put the wok on a stand. Pour in sufficient boiling water to come about 2 inches up the sides and bring back to simmering point. Carefully place the bamboo steamer in the wok so that it rests securely against the sloping sides without touching the surface of the water.

2 Cover the steamer with its matching lid and cook for the time recommended in the recipe. Check the water level from time to time and add more boiling water if necessary.

USING A WOK AS A STEAMER

1 Put a trivet in the wok, then place the wok securely on its stand. Pour in sufficient boiling water to come just below the trivet. Carefully place a plate containing the food to be steamed on the trivet.

2 Cover the wok with its lid, bring the water back to a boil, then lower the heat so that it is simmering gently. Steam for the time recommended in the recipe. Check the water level from time to time and add boiling water if necessary.

INGREDIENTS

BAMBOO SHOOTS
These mild-flavored tender shoots of the young bamboo are widely available fresh, or sliced or halved in cans.

BEAN SPROUTS
These shoots of the mung bean are usually available at supermarkets. They add a crisp texture to stir-fries.

1 Pick over the bean sprouts and discard any that are discolored, broken or wilted.

2 Rinse the bean sprouts under cold running water and drain well.

CHINESE FIVE-SPICE POWDER
This flavoring contains star anise, pepper, fennel, cloves and cinnamon.

CHINESE PANCAKES
These unseasoned flour-and-water pancakes are available fresh or frozen.

CHINESE RICE VINEGAR
There are two basic types: red vinegar is made from fermented rice and is dark colored; white vinegar is distilled from rice and has a stronger flavor.

CREAMED COCONUT
This is available in solid blocks at Asian food stores and large supermarkets. It gives an intense coconut flavor; simply add water to make a thick coconut paste. It can be thinned with more water if required.

GINGER
Ginger has a sharp, distinctive flavor. Choose firm, plump pieces of fresh root with unwrinkled, shiny skins.

1 Using a small sharp knife, peel the skin from the root.

2 Place the ginger on a board. Set the flat side of a cleaver or chef's knife on top and strike it firmly with your fist to soften its fibrous texture.

3 Chop the ginger as coarsely or finely as you wish, moving the blade backward and forward.

GRAM FLOUR
Made from ground chickpeas, this flour has a unique flavor and is worth seeking out at Indian food stores.

KAFFIR LIME LEAVES
These are used rather like bay leaves, but to give an aromatic lime flavor to dishes. The fresh leaves are available at Asian food stores and can be frozen for future use.

1 Using a small, sharp knife, remove the center vein.

2 Cut the leaves horizontally into very fine strips.

LEMONGRASS
This herb imparts a mild, sour-sweet, citrus flavor. Split and use whole, finely chopped or ground to a paste.

DAIKON
Daikon is a member of the radish family with a fresh, slightly peppery taste. Unlike other radishes, it is good when cooked, but should be salted and allowed to drain first, as it has a high water content. It is widely used in Chinese cooking and may be carved into an elaborate garnish.

OKRA
This edible seedpod is a member of the hibiscus family and is also known as bhindi, gumbo and ladies' fingers. It is widely used in Indian cuisine.

OYSTER SAUCE
Made from oyster extract, it is used in many fish dishes, soups and sauces.

PLUM SAUCE
This is a sweet-and-sour sauce with a unique fruity flavor.

RED BEAN PASTE
This reddish-brown paste is made from puréed red beans and crystallized sugar. It is usually sold in cans.

RICE
Long-grain rice is generally used for savory dishes. There are many high-quality varieties, from a range of countries. Basmati, which means "fragrant" in Hindi, is generally acknowledged as the prince or king of rices and is probably the ideal choice for Indian recipes that suggest serving the dish with rice. Thai jasmine rice is also fragrant and slightly sticky.

RICE WINE
Made from glutinous rice, Chinese rice wine is also known as yellow wine—*huang jiu* or *chiew*—because of its color. The best variety is called *shao hsing* or *shaoxing* and comes from southeast China. Dry or medium sherry may be used as substitute.

SALTED BLACK BEANS
Sold in plastic bags and jars, these very

salty and pungent beans should be crushed with water or wine before use. They will keep almost indefinitely in a screw-top jar.

SCALLIONS
These are widely used in stir-fried dishes. The thinner the onion, the milder it will be. Chop off the roots and the top part of the green section, then chop finely or cut into matchstick strips. In some recipes, the green and white parts are kept separate for an extra decorative effect.

SESAME OIL
This is used more for flavoring than for cooking. It is very intensely flavored, so only a little is required.

SHALLOTS
Mild-flavored members of the onion family, shallots are used in many flavorings and sauces, such as Thai curry paste. Fried in crisp flakes, they can be used as a garnish.

COOK'S TIP

Coconut milk is an important ingredient in Thai, Indonesian and other Southeast Asian cuisines. It is not the same as the "milk" found inside the coconut naturally, but is made from the unsweetened, grated flesh mixed with water. It is available in cans, compressed blocks or in powder form.

To make your own coconut milk, break open a fresh coconut and remove the brown inner skin from the flesh. Grate sufficient flesh to measure 1⅔ cups. Place the grated flesh, together with 1¼ cups water, in a blender or food processor fitted with a metal blade, and process for 1 minute. Strain the mixture through a strainer lined with cheesecloth into a bowl. Gather up the corners of the cloth and squeeze out the liquid. The coconut milk is then ready to use, but you should stir before using.

SOY SAUCE
Made from naturally fermented soybeans, this popular sauce is used both for cooking and at the table. Light soy sauce has more flavor than the sweeter dark soy sauce.

SPRING ROLL WRAPPERS
Paper-thin wrappers made from wheat or rice flour and water, these are available at Asian food stores. Wheat wrappers are usually sold frozen and should be thawed and separated before use. Rice flour wrappers are dry and must be soaked before use.

SZECHUAN PEPPERCORNS
Also known as *farchiew*, these aromatic red peppercorns are best used roasted and ground. They are not as hot as either white or black peppercorns, but do add a unique taste to food.

TAMARIND
This is the sticky brown pulp of the beanlike seedpod of the tamarind tree. It is used in Thai and Indonesian cooking to add tartness to recipes, rather like Western cooks use vinegar or lemon juice. It is usually sold dried or pulped. The pulp is diluted with water and strained before use. Soak 1 ounce tamarind pulp in ⅔ cup warm water for about 10 minutes. Squeeze out as much tamarind juice as possible by pressing all the liquid through a sieve.

THAI CURRY PASTES
Curry paste is traditionally made by pounding fresh herbs and spices in a mortar with a pestle. There are two types—red and green, made with red and green chilies respectively. Other ingredients vary with individual cooks, but red curry paste typically contains ginger, shallots, garlic, coriander and cumin seeds and lime juice, as well as chilies. Herbs and flavorings in green curry paste usually include scallions, fresh cilantro, kaffir lime leaves, ginger, garlic and lemongrass. Making curry paste is time-consuming, but it tastes

excellent and keeps well. Ready-made pastes, available in packages and tubs, are satisfactory substitutes.

THAI FISH SAUCE (NAM PLA)
This is used in Thai recipes in much the same way soy sauce is used in Chinese recipes.

TOFU
Also known as bean curd, tofu is bland in flavor but readily absorbs the flavors of the food with which it is cooked. Firm blocks of tofu are best suited to stir-frying. Store, covered with water, in the refrigerator.

TURMERIC
A member of the ginger family, turmeric is a rich, golden-colored root. If you are using the fresh root, wear rubber gloves when peeling it to avoid staining your skin.

WATER CHESTNUTS
These walnut-sized bulbs come from an Asian water plant and look like sweet chestnuts. They are sold fresh at some Asian food stores, but are more readily available canned.

WONTON WRAPPERS
These paper-thin squares of yellow-colored dough are available at most Asian food stores.

WILD RICE
This is not, in fact, rice at all, but a form of aquatic grass. While not a traditional, Asian "rice," it has become very popular. It takes a long time to cook—up to 50 minutes—and is often sold in combination with long-grain and basmati rice.

YELLOW BEAN SAUCE
This thick paste is made from salted, fermented yellow soybeans, crushed

Clockwise from top left: chicken stock, garam masala, fresh coconut milk, Thai red curry paste and (center) Thai green curry paste.

SOUPS AND APPETIZERS

Delicately flavored soups, crisp deep-fried spring rolls, spicy seafood and gloriously self-indulgent and sticky ribs and wings are only some of the deliciously different appetizers that can be easily and quickly prepared in a wok. Wok and stir-fry cooking can be used to full advantage for preparing the first course when entertaining, allowing you to prepare all the ingredients in advance so that you can spend time with your guests and still produce a mouthwatering start to the meal—apparently without any effort and in a matter of mere moments.

Corn and Chicken Soup

This popular, classic Chinese soup is delicious and extremely easy to make in a wok.

INGREDIENTS

Serves 4-6

1 boneless chicken breast (about 4 ounces), skinned and cubed
2 teaspoons light soy sauce
1 tablespoon Chinese rice wine or dry sherry
1 teaspoon cornstarch
¼ cup cold water
1 teaspoon sesame oil
2 tablespoons peanut oil
1 teaspoon grated fresh ginger
4 cups chicken stock
15-ounce can creamed corn
8-ounce can corn kernels
2 eggs, beaten
salt and ground black pepper
2–3 scallions, green parts only, cut into tiny rounds, to garnish

1 Grind the chicken in a food processor or blender, taking care not to overprocess. Transfer the chicken to a bowl and stir in the soy sauce, rice wine or sherry, cornstarch, water, sesame oil and seasoning. Cover and let sit for about 15 minutes to absorb the flavors.

2 Heat a wok over medium heat. Add the peanut oil and swirl it around. Add the ginger and stir-fry for a few seconds. Add the stock, creamed corn and corn kernels. Bring to just below boiling point.

3 Spoon about 6 tablespoons of the hot liquid into the chicken mixture and stir until it forms a smooth paste. Add to the wok. Slowly bring to a boil, stirring constantly, then simmer for 2–3 minutes, until cooked.

4 Pour the beaten eggs into the soup in a slow, steady stream, using a fork or chopsticks to stir the top of the soup in a figure-eight pattern. The egg should set in lacy threads. Serve immediately with the scallions sprinkled on top.

Chicken and Asparagus Soup

This is a very delicate soup, with chicken and asparagus simply and quickly prepared in a wok.

INGREDIENTS

Serves 4

1 boneless chicken breast (about 5 ounces), skinned
1 teaspoon egg white
1 teaspoon cornstarch paste
½ bunch fresh asparagus (about 4 ounces)
3 cups chicken stock
salt and ground black pepper
fresh cilantro, to garnish

1 Cut the chicken into thin slices, each about the size of a postage stamp. Mix with a pinch of salt, then add the egg white and finally the cornstarch paste.

2 Discard the tough stems of the asparagus, and cut the tender spears diagonally into short lengths.

3 Bring the stock to a rolling boil in a wok. Add the asparagus, bring back to a boil and cook for 2 minutes.

4 Add the chicken, stir to separate and bring back to a boil again. Adjust the seasoning to taste. Serve hot, garnished with fresh cilantro leaves.

Corn and Crabmeat Soup

Surprisingly, this soup originated in the United States, but it has since been introduced into mainstream Chinese cooking. It is important that you make sure you use creamed corn in the recipe to achieve exactly the right consistency.

INGREDIENTS

Serves 4

4 ounces crabmeat
½ teaspoon finely chopped fresh
  ginger
2 egg whites
2 tablespoons milk
1 tablespoon cornstarch paste
2½ cups chicken stock
8-ounce can creamed corn
salt and ground black pepper
finely chopped scallions, to garnish

1 Flake the crabmeat roughly with chopsticks. Mix the crabmeat with the chopped ginger.

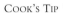

—— COOK'S TIP ——

The crabmeat can be replaced with chopped boneless chicken breast.

2 Beat the egg whites until frothy, add the milk and cornstarch paste and beat again until smooth. Blend with the crabmeat.

3 Bring the stock to a boil in a wok. Add the creamed corn and bring back to a boil again.

4 Stir in the crabmeat and egg white mixture, adjust the seasoning and simmer gently until cooked. Serve garnished with finely chopped scallions.

Hot-and-sour Soup

This surely must be the best-known and all-time favorite soup in Chinese restaurants throughout the world. It is fairly simple to make once you have all the necessary ingredients together.

INGREDIENTS

Serves 4

4–6 dried Chinese mushrooms, soaked in warm water for 30 minutes
4 ounces pork or chicken
8-ounce package fresh tofu
⅓ cup sliced bamboo shoots, drained
2½ cups chicken stock
1 tablespoon Chinese rice wine or dry sherry
1 tablespoon light soy sauce
1 tablespoon rice vinegar
salt and ground white pepper
1 tablespoon cornstarch paste

1 Drain the mushrooms, squeezing out the excess moisture, then discard the hard stalks. Thinly shred the mushrooms, meat, tofu and bamboo shoots.

2 Bring the stock to a rolling boil in a wok and add the shredded ingredients. Bring back to a boil and simmer for about 1 minute.

3 Add the wine or sherry, soy sauce and vinegar and season. Bring back to a boil, then add the cornstarch paste, stir until thickened and serve.

Spinach and Tofu Soup

If fresh young spinach leaves are not available, watercress or lettuce can be used instead. Sorrel leaves may also be used as a substitute, but they have a stronger and slightly more bitter flavor than spinach.

INGREDIENTS

Serves 4
3-inch block fresh tofu
½ bunch spinach
3 cups chicken stock
1 tablespoon light soy sauce
salt and ground black pepper

1 Cut the tofu into 12 small pieces, each about ¼ inch thick. Wash the spinach leaves and cut them into small pieces.

2 Bring the stock to a rolling boil in a wok. Add the tofu and soy sauce, bring back to a boil and simmer for about 2 minutes.

3 Add the spinach and simmer for another minute. Skim the surface to make it clear, then adjust the seasoning and serve immediately.

--- COOK'S TIP ---

Fresh tofu is sold in cakes about 3 inches square in Asian food stores. Do not confuse it with fermented tofu, which is much stronger-tasting, quite salty and usually used as a condiment.

Sliced Fish and Cilantro Soup

It is not necessary to remove the skin from the fish; it helps to keep the flesh together when poached in the wok.

INGREDIENTS

Serves 4
8 ounces white fish fillets, such as lemon sole or flounder
1 tablespoon egg white
2 teaspoons cornstarch paste
3 cups chicken stock
1 tablespoon light soy sauce
½ cup chopped fresh cilantro
salt and ground black pepper

1 Cut the fish into slices, each about 1½ inches square. Mix with the egg white and cornstarch paste.

2 Bring the stock to a rolling boil in a wok and poach the fish slices for about 1 minute.

3 Add the soy sauce and chopped cilantro, adjust the seasoning and serve immediately.

Three-delicacy Soup

This delicious soup combines the three ingredients chicken, ham and shrimp.

INGREDIENTS

Serves 4
4 ounces boneless chicken breast
4 ounces honey-roast ham
4 ounces shelled shrimp
3 cups chicken stock
salt

COOK'S TIP

Fresh, uncooked shrimp impart the best flavor. If these are not available, you can use cooked shrimp. They must be added at the last stage to prevent over-cooking.

1 Thinly slice the chicken and ham into small pieces. Devein the shrimp and, if they are large, cut each in half lengthwise.

2 Bring the stock to a rolling boil in a wok. Add the chicken, ham and shrimp. Bring back to a boil, add salt and simmer for 1 minute. Serve the soup hot.

Lamb and Cucumber Soup

This is a variation on hot-and-sour soup, but it is even simpler to prepare.

INGREDIENTS

Serves 4
8 ounces lamb steak
1 tablespoon light soy sauce
1 tablespoon Chinese rice wine or
  dry sherry
½ teaspoon sesame oil
3-inch piece cucumber
3 cups chicken stock
1 tablespoon rice vinegar
salt and ground white pepper

1 Trim off any excess fat from the lamb and discard. Thinly slice the lamb into small pieces. Put it in a shallow dish and add the soy sauce, rice wine or sherry and sesame oil. Set aside to marinate for 25–30 minutes. Discard the marinade.

2 Halve the cucumber piece lengthwise (do not peel), then cut it into thin slices diagonally.

3 Bring the stock to a rolling boil in a wok. Add the lamb and stir to separate. Return to a boil, then add the cucumber slices, vinegar and seasoning. Bring to a boil again, and serve immediately.

Wonton Soup

In China, wonton soup is served as a snack or dim sum rather than as a soup course during a large meal.

INGREDIENTS

Serves 4

6 ounces pork, not too lean, roughly chopped
8 medium shrimp, shelled and ground
1 teaspoon light brown sugar
1 tablespoon Chinese rice wine or dry sherry
2 tablespoons light soy sauce
1 teaspoon finely chopped scallion
1 teaspoon finely chopped fresh ginger
24 wonton wrappers
3 cups chicken stock
finely chopped scallions, to garnish

1 In a bowl, mix the chopped pork and ground shrimp with the sugar, rice wine or sherry, 1 tablespoon of the soy sauce, the scallions and chopped ginger. Blend well and set aside for 25–30 minutes for the flavors to blend.

2 Place 1 teaspoon of the filling in the center of each wonton wrapper.

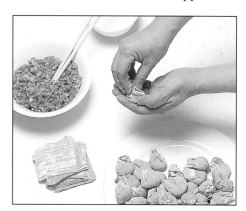

3 Wet the edges of each wonton with a little water and press them together with your fingers to seal, then fold each wonton over.

4 To cook, bring the stock to a rolling boil in a wok, add the wontons and cook for 4–5 minutes. Add the remaining soy sauce and scallions, transfer to individual soup bowls and serve.

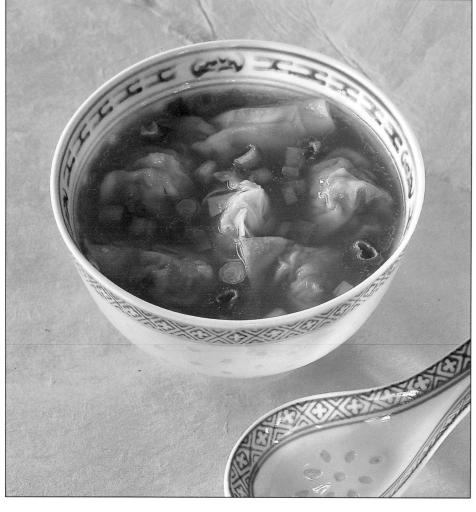

Fried Wontons

These delicious vegetarian versions of the classic wontons are filled with bean curd, scallions, garlic and ginger.

INGREDIENTS

Makes 30
30 wonton wrappers
1 egg, beaten
oil for deep-frying

For the filling
2 teaspoons vegetable oil
1 tablespoon grated fresh ginger
2 garlic cloves, finely chopped
8 ounces firm bean curd (tofu)
6 scallions, finely chopped
2 teaspoons sesame oil
1 tablespoon soy sauce
salt and freshly ground black pepper

For the dipping sauce
2 tablespoons soy sauce
1 tablespoon sesame oil
1 tablespoon rice vinegar
½ teaspoon chili oil
½ teaspoon honey
2 tablespoons water

1 Line a large baking sheet with wax paper, or sprinkle lightly with flour, then set aside. To make the filling, heat the oil in a frying pan. Add the fresh ginger and garlic cloves, and fry for 30 seconds. Crumble in the bean curd, and stir-fry for a few minutes.

2 Add the scallions, sesame oil and soy sauce to the pan. Stir well, and taste for seasoning. Remove from the heat. Set aside to cool.

3 Make the dipping sauce by combining all the ingredients in a bowl and mixing well.

4 Place a wonton wrapper on a board in a diamond position. Brush the edges lightly with beaten egg. Spoon 1 teaspoon of the filling on the center of the wonton wrapper.

5 Pull the top corner down to the bottom corner, folding the wrapper over the filling to make a triangle. Press firmly to seal. Place on the prepared baking sheet. Repeat with the rest of the wonton wrappers.

6 Heat the oil in a deep-fryer or large saucepan. Carefully add the wontons, a few at a time, and cook for a few minutes until golden brown. Drain on paper towels, then serve at once with the dipping sauce.

Pork Dumplings

These dumplings, when shallow-fried, make a good first course to a multicourse meal. They can also be steamed and served as a snack or poached in large quantities for a complete meal.

INGREDIENTS

Makes about 80–90
2½ cups all-purpose flour, plus extra
   for dusting
2 cups water
salt

For the filling
1 pound bok choy leaves or white
   cabbage
1 pound ground pork
1 tablespoon finely chopped scallions
1 teaspoon finely chopped fresh ginger
2 teaspoons salt
1 teaspoon light brown sugar
2 tablespoons light soy sauce
1 tablespoon Chinese rice wine or
   dry sherry
2 teaspoons sesame oil

For the dipping sauce
2 tablespoons red chili oil
1 tablespoon light soy sauce
1 teaspoon finely chopped garlic
1 tablespoon finely chopped scallions

1 Sift the flour into a bowl, then pour in the water and mix to a firm dough. Knead until smooth on a lightly floured surface, then cover with a damp cloth and set aside for 25–30 minutes.

2 For the filling, blanch the bok choy until soft. Drain and chop finely. Mix the bok choy with the pork, scallions, ginger, salt, sugar, soy sauce, wine or sherry and sesame oil.

3 Lightly dust a work surface with flour. Knead and roll the dough into a long sausage about 1 inch in diameter. Cut the sausage into 80–90 small pieces and flatten each piece with the palm of your hand.

4 Using a rolling pin, roll out each piece into a thin pancake about 2½ inches in diameter.

5 Place about 1⅓ tablespoons of the filling in the center of each pancake and fold into a half-moon pouch.

6 Pinch the edges firmly so that the dumpling is tightly sealed.

7 Bring ⅔ cup salted water to a boil in a wok. Add the dumplings and poach for 2 minutes. Remove the wok from the heat and leave the dumplings in the water for another 15 minutes.

8 Make the dipping sauce by combining all the sauce ingredients in a bowl and mixing well. Serve in a small bowl with the dumplings.

Thai Spring Rolls

These crunchy spring rolls are as popular in Thai cuisine as they are in the Chinese. Thais fill their version with a garlic, pork and noodle filling.

INGREDIENTS

Makes about 24

4–6 dried Chinese mushrooms, soaked
2 ounces bean thread noodles, soaked
2 tablespoons vegetable oil
2 garlic cloves, chopped
2 red chilies, seeded and chopped
8 ounces ground pork
2 ounces chopped cooked shrimp
2 tablespoons fish sauce
1 teaspoon sugar
1 carrot, finely shredded
2 ounces bamboo shoots, chopped
¼ cup bean sprouts
2 scallions, chopped
1 tablespoon chopped cilantro
2 tablespoons flour
24 × 6-inch square spring roll wrappers
freshly ground black pepper
oil for frying

1 Drain and chop the mushrooms. Drain the noodles and cut into short lengths of about 2 inches.

2 Heat the oil in a wok or frying pan, add the garlic and chilies and fry for 30 seconds. Add the pork, stirring until the meat is browned.

3 Add the noodles, mushrooms and shrimp. Season with fish sauce, sugar and pepper. Turn into a bowl.

4 Mix in the carrot, bamboo shoots, bean sprouts, scallions and chopped cilantro for the filling.

5 Put the flour in a small bowl and mix with a little water to make a paste. Place a spoonful of filling in the center of a spring roll wrapper.

6 Turn the bottom edge over to cover the filling, then fold in the left and right sides. Roll the wrapper up almost to the top edge. Brush the top edge with flour paste and seal. Repeat with the rest of the wrappers.

7 Heat the oil in a wok or deep-fat fryer. Slide in the spring rolls a few at a time and fry until crisp and golden brown. Remove with a slotted spoon and drain on paper towels. Serve hot with Thai sweet chili sauce to dip them into, if you like.

Vietnamese Spring Rolls with Nuoc Cham Sauce

INGREDIENTS

Makes 25
6 dried Chinese mushrooms, soaked
   in hot water for 30 minutes
8 ounces lean ground pork
4 ounces uncooked shrimp, peeled,
   deveined and chopped
4 ounces white crabmeat, picked over
1 carrot, shredded
2 ounces cellophane noodles, soaked
   in water, drained and cut into
   short lengths
4 scallions, finely sliced
2 garlic cloves, finely chopped
2 tablespoons fish sauce
juice of 1 lime
freshly ground black pepper
25 x 4-inch Vietnamese rice sheets
oil for deep-frying
lettuce leaves, cucumber slices and
   cilantro leaves, to garnish

For the nuoc cham sauce
2 garlic cloves, finely chopped
2 tablespoons white wine vinegar
juice of 1 lime
2 tablespoons sugar
½ cup fish sauce
½ cup water
2 red chilies, seeded and chopped

1 Drain the mushrooms, squeezing out the excess moisture. Remove the stems, and thinly slice the caps into a bowl. Add the pork, shrimp, crabmeat, carrot, cellophane noodles, scallions and garlic.

2 Season with the fish sauce, lime juice and pepper. Set the mixture aside for about 30 minutes to allow the flavors to blend.

3 Meanwhile, make the nuoc cham sauce. Mix together the garlic, vinegar, lime juice, sugar, fish sauce, water and chilies in a serving bowl, then cover and set aside.

4 Assemble the spring rolls. Place a rice sheet on a flat surface, and brush with warm water until it is pliable. Place about 2 teaspoons of the filling near the edge of the rice sheet. Fold the sides over the filling, fold in the two ends, then roll up, sealing the ends of the roll with a little water. Make more rolls in the same way until all the filling is used up.

5 Heat the oil for deep-frying to 350°F or until a cube of dry bread added to the oil browns in about 30–45 seconds. Add the rolls, a few at a time, and fry until golden brown and crisp. Drain on paper towels. Serve the spring rolls hot, garnished with the lettuce, cucumber and cilantro. Offer the nuoc cham sauce separately.

Chinese Crispy Spring Rolls

These dainty vegetarian stir-fried rolls are ideal served as appetizers or cocktail snacks. For a heartier version replace the mushrooms with chicken or pork, and substitute shrimp for the carrots.

Ingredients

Makes about 40

1 cup bean sprouts
1 bunch scallions
2 carrots
⅔ cup bamboo shoots, sliced
1½ cups white mushrooms
3–4 tablespoons vegetable oil
1 teaspoon salt
1 teaspoon light brown sugar
1 tablespoon light soy sauce
1 tablespoon Chinese rice wine or
    dry sherry
about 40 spring roll wrappers
1 tablespoon cornstarch paste
flour, for dusting
oil, for deep-frying
soy sauce, to serve (optional)

1 Cut all the vegetables into thin shreds, roughly the same size and shape as the bean sprouts.

COOK'S TIP

To make cornstarch paste, mix 4 parts dry cornstarch with about 5 parts cold water until smooth.

---

2 Heat the oil in a wok and stir-fry the vegetables for about 1 minute. Add the salt, sugar, soy sauce and rice wine or sherry and stir-fry for 1½–2 minutes. Remove and drain the excess liquid, then let cool.

3 To make the spring rolls, cut each wrapper in half diagonally, then place about 1 tablespoon of the vegetable mixture one-third of the way down on the wrapper, with the triangle pointing away from you.

4 Lift the lower flap over the filling and roll it up once.

5 Fold in both ends and roll once more, then brush the upper edge with a little cornstarch paste, and roll into a neat package. Lightly dust a baking sheet with flour and place the spring rolls on the baking sheet with the flap side down.

6 To cook, heat the oil in a wok until hot, then reduce the heat to low. Deep-fry the spring rolls in batches (about 8–10 at a time) for 2–3 minutes, or until golden and crisp, then remove and drain. Serve the spring rolls hot with soy sauce, if desired.

Butterfly Shrimp

For best results, use uncooked jumbo shrimp in their shells for this deep-fried dish. Sold headless, they are about 3–4 inches long, and you should get 18–20 shrimp per pound.

INGREDIENTS

Serves 6–8

1 pound uncooked shrimp in their shells, heads removed
1 teaspoon ground Szechuan peppercorns
1 tablespoon light soy sauce
1 tablespoon Chinese rice wine or dry sherry
2 teaspoons cornstarch
2 eggs, lightly beaten
4–5 tablespoons bread crumbs
vegetable oil, for deep-frying
2–3 scallions, to garnish
lettuce leaves, to serve

1 Shell the shrimp but leave the tails on. Butterfly the shrimp, about three-quarters of the way through their length, leaving the tails still firmly attached.

2 Put the shrimp in a bowl with the pepper, soy sauce, rice wine or sherry and cornstarch and set aside to marinate for 10–15 minutes.

3 Pick up one shrimp at a time by the tail, and dip it in the beaten egg.

4 Roll the egg-covered shrimp in bread crumbs.

5 Heat the oil in a wok until medium-hot. Gently lower the shrimp into the oil.

6 Deep-fry the shrimp in batches until golden brown. Remove and drain. To serve, arrange the shrimp neatly on a bed of lettuce leaves. Garnish with scallions, either raw or after soaking for about 30 seconds in hot oil.

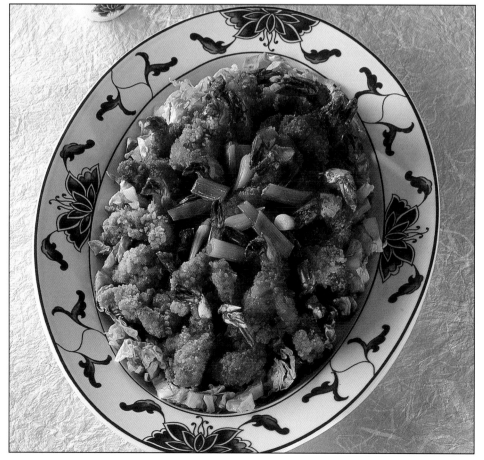

Quick-fried Shrimp with Hot Spices

These spicy shrimp are stir-fried in moments to make a wonderful appetizer. Don't forget that you will need to provide your guests with finger bowls.

INGREDIENTS

Serves 4

1 pound uncooked large shrimp
1-inch piece fresh ginger, grated
2 garlic cloves, crushed
1 teaspoon hot chili powder
1 teaspoon ground turmeric
2 teaspoons black mustard seeds
seeds from 4 green cardamom pods, crushed
4 tablespoons ghee or butter
$^1/_2$ cup coconut milk
salt and ground black pepper
2–3 tablespoons chopped fresh cilantro, to garnish
naan, to serve

1 Shell the shrimp carefully, leaving the tails attached.

2 Using a small, sharp knife, make a slit along the back of each shrimp and remove the dark vein. Rinse under cold running water, drain and pat dry.

3 Put the ginger, garlic, chili powder, turmeric, mustard seeds and cardamom seeds in a bowl. Add the shrimp and toss to coat completely with spice mixture.

4 Heat a wok until hot. Add the ghee or butter and swirl it around until foaming.

5 Add the marinated shrimp and stir-fry for 1–1½ minutes, until they are just turning pink.

6 Stir in the coconut milk and simmer for 3–4 minutes, until the shrimp are just cooked through. Season to taste with salt and pepper. Sprinkle the cilantro on top and serve immediately with naan.

Deep-fried Ribs with Spicy Salt and Pepper

INGREDIENTS

Serves 4–6

10–12 pork spareribs (about 1½ pounds), excess fat trimmed
2–3 tablespoons flour
vegetable oil, for deep-frying
scallion tassels, to garnish (optional)

For the marinade

1 clove garlic, crushed
1 tablespoon light brown sugar
1 tablespoon light soy sauce
1 tablespoon dark soy sauce
2 tablespoons Chinese rice wine or
   dry sherry
½ teaspoon chili sauce
few drops of sesame oil

For the spicy salt and pepper

1 tablespoon salt
2 teaspoons ground Szechuan
   peppercorns
1 teaspoon five-spice powder

1 Chop each rib into three or four pieces, then mix with all the marinade ingredients and marinate for at least 2–3 hours.

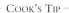

> — COOK'S TIP —
>
> Ideally, each sparerib should be chopped into three or four bite-size pieces before or after deep-frying in a wok. If this is not possible, serve the ribs whole.

2 Coat the ribs with flour and deep-fry in medium-hot oil for 4–5 minutes, stirring to separate. Remove from the oil and drain.

3 Heat the oil to high and deep-fry the ribs again for about 1 minute or until the color is an even dark brown. Remove and drain.

4 To make the spicy salt and pepper, heat all the ingredients in a preheated dry wok for about 2 minutes over low heat, stirring constantly. Serve with the ribs. Garnish the dish with scallion tassels, if desired.

Deep-fried Squid with Spicy Salt and Pepper

This recipe is one of the specialities of the Cantonese school of cuisine. Southern China is famous for its seafood, often flavored with ginger.

INGREDIENTS

Serves 4

1 pound squid
1 teaspoon ginger juice (see Cook's Tip)
1 tablespoon Chinese rice wine or dry sherry
about 2½ cups boiling water
vegetable oil, for deep-frying
spicy salt and pepper (see index)
fresh cilantro leaves, to garnish

1 Clean the squid by discarding the head and the transparent backbone as well as the ink bag; peel off and discard the thin skin, then wash the squid and dry well on paper towels. Open up the squid and, using a sharp knife, score the inside of the flesh in a crisscross pattern.

2 Cut the squid into pieces, each about the size of a postage stamp. Marinate in a bowl with the ginger juice and rice wine or sherry for 25–30 minutes.

3 Blanch the squid in boiling water for a few seconds—each piece will curl up and the crisscross pattern will open out to resemble ears of corn. Remove and drain. Dry well.

4 Heat sufficient oil for deep-frying in a wok. Deep-fry the squid for 15–20 seconds, remove quickly and drain. Sprinkle with the spicy salt and pepper and serve garnished with fresh cilantro leaves.

--- COOK'S TIP ---

To make ginger juice, mix finely chopped or grated fresh ginger with an equal quantity of cold water and place in a piece of damp cheesecloth. Twist tightly to extract the juice. Alternatively, crush the ginger in a garlic press.

Spicy Meat-filled Packages

In Indonesia the finest gossamer dough is made for *Martabak*. You can achieve equally good results using ready-made filo pastry or spring roll wrappers.

INGREDIENTS

Makes 16
1 pound lean ground beef
2 small onions, finely chopped
2 small leeks, very
  finely chopped
2 garlic cloves, crushed
2 teaspoons coriander seeds, dry-fried
  and ground
1 teaspoon cumin seeds, dry-fried
  and ground
1–2 teaspoons mild curry powder
2 eggs, beaten
1-pound package filo pastry
3–4 tablespoons sunflower oil
salt and freshly ground black pepper
light soy sauce, to serve

1 To make the filling, mix the meat with the onions, leeks, garlic, coriander, cumin, curry powder and seasoning. Turn into a heated wok, without oil, and stir constantly, until the meat has changed color and looks cooked, about 5 minutes.

2 Allow to cool and then mix in enough beaten egg to bind to a soft consistency. Any leftover egg can be used to seal the edges of the dough; otherwise, use milk.

3 Brush a sheet of filo with oil and lay another sheet on top. Cut the sheets in half. Place a large spoonful of the filling on each double piece of filo. Fold the sides to the middle so that the edges just overlap. Brush these edges with either beaten egg or milk and fold the other two sides to the middle in the same way, so that you now have a square package. Make sure that the package is as flat as possible, to speed cooking. Repeat with the other fifteen packages and place on a floured sheet of wax paper on a tray in the fridge.

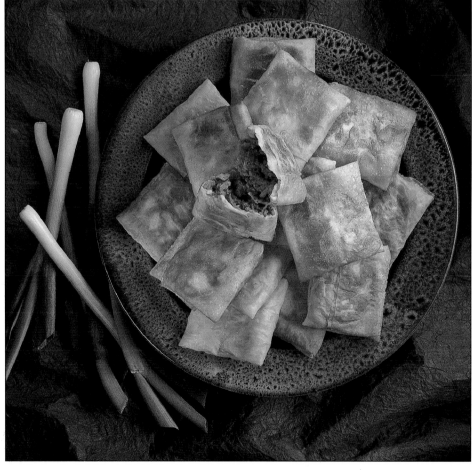

4 Heat the remaining oil in a shallow pan and cook several packages at a time, depending on the size of the pan. Cook for 3 minutes on the first side and then turn them over and cook for another 2 minutes, or until heated through. Cook the remaining packages in the same way and serve hot, sprinkled with light soy sauce.

5 If preferred, these spicy packages can be cooked in a hot oven at 400°F for 20 minutes. Glaze with more beaten egg before baking for a rich, golden color.

Hot and Spicy Crab Claws

Crab claws are used to delicious effect in this quick stir-fried appetizer based on an Indonesian dish called *kepiting pedas*.

INGREDIENTS

Serves 4
12 fresh or frozen and thawed cooked
  crab claws
4 shallots, roughly chopped
2–4 fresh red chilies, seeded and
  roughly chopped
3 garlic cloves, roughly chopped
1 teaspoon grated fresh ginger
$1/2$ teaspoon ground coriander
3 tablespoons peanut oil
$1/4$ cup water
2 teaspoons sweet soy sauce
2–3 teaspoons lime juice
salt
fresh cilantro leaves, to garnish

1 Crack the crab claws with the back of a heavy knife to make eating them easier and set aside. In a mortar, pound the chopped shallots with the pestle until pulpy. Add the chilies, garlic, ginger and ground coriander and pound until the mixture forms a fairly coarse paste.

2 Heat the wok over medium heat. Add the oil and swirl it around. When it is hot, stir in the chili paste. Stir-fry for about 30 seconds. Increase the heat to high. Add the crab claws and stir-fry for another 3–4 minutes.

3 Stir in the water, sweet soy sauce, lime juice and salt to taste. Continue to stir-fry for 1–2 minutes. Serve immediately, garnished with fresh cilantro. The crab claws are eaten with the fingers, so it is helpful to provide finger bowls.

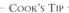
COOK'S TIP

If whole crab claws are unavailable, look for frozen ready prepared crab claws. These are shelled, with just the tip of the claw attached to the whole meat. Stir-fry for about 2 minutes, until heated through.

Crispy "Seaweed"

Surprisingly, the very popular and rather exotic-sounding "seaweed" served in Chinese restaurants is, in fact, just ordinary spring greens.

INGREDIENTS

Serves 4

1 pound collards or spring greens
vegetable oil, for deep-frying
¹/₂ teaspoon salt
1 teaspoon superfine sugar
1 tablespoon ground fried fish, to
 garnish (optional)

1 Cut out the hard stalks in the center of each spring green leaf. Pile the leaves on top of each other, and roll into a tight sausage shape. Thinly cut the leaves into fine shreds. Spread them out to dry.

2 Heat the oil in a wok until hot. Deep-fry the shredded greens in batches, stirring to separate them.

3 Remove the greens with a slotted spoon as soon as they are crispy, but before they turn brown. Drain. Sprinkle the salt and sugar evenly all over the "seaweed," mix well, garnish with ground fish, if desired, and serve.

Sesame Seed Shrimp Toasts

Use uncooked shrimp for this dish, as cooked ones will tend to separate from the bread during cooking.

INGREDIENTS

Serves 4

8 ounces uncooked shrimp, shelled
1 tablespoon vegetable shortening
1 egg white, lightly beaten
1 teaspoon finely chopped scallions
¹/₂ teaspoon finely chopped fresh
 ginger
1 tablespoon Chinese rice wine or
 dry sherry
1 tablespoon cornstarch paste
1 cup white sesame seeds
6 large slices white bread
vegetable oil, for deep-frying
salt and ground black pepper

1 Chop the shrimp with the shortening to form a smooth paste. In a bowl, mix with all the other ingredients except the sesame seeds and bread.

2 Spread the sesame seeds evenly on a large plate or baking sheet; spread the shrimp paste thickly on one side of each slice of bread, then press, spread side down, onto the seeds.

3 Heat the oil in a wok until medium-hot; fry 2–3 slices of the sesame bread at a time, spread side down, for 2–3 minutes. Remove and drain. Cut each slice into six or eight fingers (without crusts).

Sweet Potato and Pumpkin Shrimp Cakes

Serve these fried cakes warm
with Thai fish sauce.

INGREDIENTS

Serves 4–6

1½ cups all-purpose flour
½ teaspoon salt
½ teaspoon active dry yeast
¾ cup warm water
1 egg, beaten
8 ounces uncooked shrimp, shelled
1 small sweet potato, peeled
 and grated
1 small wedge pumpkin (about 8
 ounces), peeled, seeded and grated
2 scallions, chopped
¼ cup water chestnuts, sliced
 and chopped
½ teaspoon chili sauce
1 clove garlic, crushed
juice of ½ lime
2–3 tablespoons vegetable oil
scallion tassel, to garnish

1 Sift the flour and salt into a mixing
bowl and make a well in the center.
Dissolve the yeast in the water, then
pour into the well. Pour in the egg and
leave for a few minutes, until bubbles
appear. Mix to a batter.

2 Place the shelled shrimp in a
saucepan and cover with water.
Bring to a boil and simmer for
10–12 minutes. Drain, refresh in cold
water and drain again. Roughly chop
and set the shrimp aside.

3 Add the sweet potato and pumpkin
to the batter, then add the scallions,
water chestnuts, chili sauce, garlic,
lime juice and shrimp. Heat a little oil
in a wok or frying pan. Spoon in the
batter in small heaps and fry until
golden. Drain and serve, garnished
with a scallion tassel.

Fish Cakes with Cucumber Relish

These wonderful small fish cakes are a very familiar and popular appetizer. They are usually accompanied by Thai beer.

INGREDIENTS

Makes about 12
11 ounces white fish fillet, such as cod, cut into chunks
2 tablespoons red curry paste
1 egg
2 tablespoons fish sauce
1 teaspoon sugar
2 tablespoons cornstarch
3 kaffir lime leaves, shredded
1 tablespoon chopped cilantro
2 ounces green beans, finely sliced
oil for frying
Chinese mustard cress, to garnish

For the cucumber relish
4 tablespoons Thai coconut or rice vinegar
4 tablespoons water
4 tablespoons sugar
1 head pickled garlic
1 cucumber, quartered and sliced
4 shallots, finely sliced
1 tablespoon finely chopped ginger
2 red chilies, seeded and finely sliced

1 For the cucumber relish, bring the vinegar, water and sugar to a boil. Stir until the sugar dissolves, remove from the heat and cool.

2 Combine the rest of the relish ingredients together in a bowl and pour over the vinegar mixture.

3 Combine the fish, curry paste and egg in a food processor and process well. Transfer the mixture to a bowl, add the rest of the ingredients, except for the oil and garnish, and mix well.

4 Mold and shape the mixture into cakes about 2 inches in diameter and ¼ inch thick.

5 Heat the oil in a wok or deep-fat fryer. Fry the fish cakes, a few at a time, for about 4–5 minutes or until golden brown. Remove and drain on paper towels. Garnish with Chinese mustard cress and serve with the cucumber relish.

Son-in-law Eggs

This fascinating name comes from a story about a prospective bridegroom who wanted to impress his future mother-in-law and devised a recipe from the only other dish he knew how to make – cooked eggs. The hard-cooked eggs are deep fried and then drenched with a sweet, piquant tamarind sauce.

INGREDIENTS

Serves 4–6

scant ½ cup palm sugar
5 tablespoons fish sauce
6 tablespoons tamarind juice
oil for frying
6 shallots, finely sliced
6 garlic cloves, finely sliced
6 red chilies, sliced
6 hard-cooked eggs, shelled
lettuce, to serve
sprigs of cilantro, to garnish

1 Combine the palm sugar, fish sauce and tamarind juice in a small saucepan. Bring to a boil, stirring until the sugar dissolves, then simmer for about 5 minutes.

2 Taste and add more palm sugar, fish sauce or tamarind juice, if necessary. It should be sweet, salty and slightly sour. Transfer the sauce to a bowl and set aside.

3 Heat the oil in a wok or deep-fat fryer. Meanwhile, heat a couple of spoonfuls of the oil in a frying pan and fry the shallots, garlic and chilies until golden brown. Transfer the mixture to a bowl and set aside.

4 Deep-fry the eggs in the oil for about 3–5 minutes, until golden brown. Remove and drain on paper towels. Cut the eggs in quarters and arrange on a bed of lettuce. Drizzle with the sauce and sprinkle over the shallots. Garnish with sprigs of cilantro.

Fried Clams with Chili and Yellow Bean Sauce

Seafood is abundant in Thailand, especially at all of the beach holiday resorts. This delicious dish, which is simple to prepare, is one of the favorites.

INGREDIENTS

Serves 4–6

2¼ pounds fresh clams
2 tablespoons vegetable oil
4 garlic cloves, finely chopped
1 tablespoon grated ginger
4 shallots, finely chopped
2 tablespoons yellow bean sauce
6 red chilies, seeded and chopped
1 tablespoon fish sauce
pinch of sugar
handful of basil leaves, plus extra
    to garnish

1 Wash and scrub the clams. Heat the oil in a wok or large frying pan. Add the garlic and ginger and fry for 30 seconds, add the shallots and fry for another minute.

2 Add the clams. Using a fish slice or spatula, turn them a few times to coat with the oil. Add the yellow bean sauce and half the red chilies.

3 Continue to cook, stirring often, for about 5–7 minutes until all the clams open. You may need to add a splash of water. Adjust the seasoning with fish sauce and a little sugar.

4 Finally add the basil and transfer to individual bowls or a platter. Garnish with the remaining red chilies and basil leaves.

Spiced Honey Chicken Wings

Be prepared to get very sticky when you eat these stir-fried chicken wings, as the best way to enjoy them is by eating them with your fingers. Provide individual finger bowls for your guests.

INGREDIENTS

Serves 4

1 red chili, finely chopped
1 teaspoon chili powder
1 teaspoon ground ginger
finely grated zest of 1 lime
12 chicken wings
¼ cup sunflower oil
1 tablespoon fresh cilantro, chopped
2 tablespoons soy sauce
4 tablespoons honey
lime zest and fresh cilantro sprigs,
    to garnish (optional)

1 Combine the fresh chili, chili powder, ground ginger and lime rind. Rub the mixture into the chicken skins and let sit for at least 2 hours to let the flavors penetrate.

2 Heat a wok and add half the oil. When the oil is hot, add half the wings and stir-fry for 10 minutes, turning regularly, until crisp and golden. Drain on paper towels. Repeat with the remaining oil and chicken wings.

3 Add the cilantro to the hot wok and stir-fry for 30 seconds, then return the wings to the wok and stir-fry for 1 minute.

4 Stir in the soy sauce and honey, and stir-fry for 1 minute. Serve the chicken wings hot with the sauce drizzled over them. Garnish with lime zest and cilantro, if wished.

Bon-bon Chicken with Sesame Sauce

The chicken meat is tenderized by being beaten with a stick (called a *bon* in Chinese), hence the name for this very popular Szechuan dish.

INGREDIENTS

Serves 6–8
1 chicken (about 3 pounds)
5 cups water
1 tablespoon sesame oil
shredded cucumber, to garnish

For the sauce
2 tablespoons light soy sauce
1 teaspoon sugar
1 tablespoon finely chopped scallions
1 teaspoon red chili oil
$1/2$ teaspoon ground Szechuan
    peppercorns
1 teaspoon white sesame seeds
2 tablespoons tahini or 2 tablespoons
    peanut butter creamed with a little
    sesame oil

1 Clean the chicken well. Bring the water to a rolling boil in a wok and add the chicken. Reduce the heat, cover and cook for 40–45 minutes. Remove the chicken and immerse in cold water to cool.

2 After at least 1 hour, remove the chicken and drain; dry well with paper towels and brush on a coating of sesame oil. Carve the meat off the legs, wings and breast and pull the meat off the rest of the bones.

3 On a flat surface, pound the meat with a rolling pin, then tear it into shreds with your fingers.

4 Place the meat in a dish with the shredded cucumber around the edge. In a bowl, combine all the sauce ingredients, keeping the scallions to garnish. Pour the sauce over the chicken, garnish and serve.

FISH AND SEAFOOD

Rapid stir-frying is ideally suited to fish and seafood, as it helps to retain their light texture and delicate flavor. This has long been an open secret in India, China and Southeast Asia, whose cuisines have inspired many of the delicious recipes here, including Indian Seafood with Vegetables, Fish Balls with Chinese Greens, Malaysian Fish Curry and Asian Scallops with Ginger Relish. A wok is also the perfect piece of equipment for braising whole fish or fillets and for preparing pastes, flavorings and sauces to accompany fish.

Fish Balls with Chinese Greens

These tasty fish balls are steamed over a wok with a selection of green vegetables—bok choy is widely available.

INGREDIENTS

Serves 4

For the fish balls
1 pound white fish fillets, skinned, boned and cubed
3 scallions, chopped
1 slice bacon, chopped
1 tablespoon Chinese rice wine or dry sherry
2 tablespoons light soy sauce
1 egg white
fresh cilantro, to garnish

For the vegetables
1 small head bok choy
1 teaspoon cornstarch
1 tablespoon light soy sauce
$^2/_3$ cup fish stock
2 tablespoons peanut oil
2 garlic cloves, sliced
1-inch piece fresh ginger, cut into shreds
$^1/_2$ cup green beans
$^3/_4$ cup snow peas
3 scallions, sliced diagonally into 2–3-inch lengths
salt and ground black pepper

1 Put the fish, scallions, bacon, wine or sherry, soy sauce and egg white in a food processor and process until smooth. With wet hands, form the mixture into about 24 small balls.

2 Steam the fish balls in batches in a lightly greased bamboo steamer in a wok for 5–10 minutes, until cooked through and firm. Remove from the steamer and keep warm.

3 Meanwhile trim the bok choy, removing any discolored leaves or damaged stems, then tear into manageable pieces.

4 Combine the cornstarch, soy sauce and stock in a small bowl and set aside.

5 Heat a wok until hot, add the oil and swirl it around. Add the garlic and ginger and stir-fry for 2–3 minutes. Add the beans and stir-fry for 2–3 minutes, then add the snow peas, scallions and bok choy. Stir-fry for 2–3 minutes.

6 Add the sauce to the wok and cook, stirring, until it has thickened and the vegetables are tender but crisp. Taste and adjust the seasoning, if necessary. Garnish the fish balls with fresh cilantro and serve with the vegetables.

COOK'S TIP

You can replace the snow peas and green beans with broccoli florets. Blanch them before stir-frying.

Thai Fish Stir-fry

This is a substantial dish, best served with crusty bread for mopping up all the spicy juices.

INGREDIENTS

Serves 4
1¹/₂ pounds mixed seafood, such as red
    snapper and cod, filleted and skinned,
    and raw shrimp
1¹/₄ cups coconut milk
1 tablespoon vegetable oil
salt and ground black pepper
crusty bread, to serve

For the sauce
2 large red fresh chilies
1 onion, roughly chopped
2-inch piece fresh ginger, peeled
    and sliced
2-inch piece lemongrass, outer leaf
    discarded, roughly sliced
2-inch piece galangal, peeled and sliced
6 blanched almonds, chopped
¹/₂ teaspoon ground turmeric
¹/₂ teaspoon salt

1 Cut the filleted fish into large chunks. Peel the shrimp, keeping their tails intact.

COOK'S TIP

Galangal, also spelled galingale, is a rhizome from the same family as ginger, with a similar but milder flavor. It is peeled and sliced, chopped or grated in the same way as ginger. It is an important ingredient in Southeast Asian cooking, particularly in Indonesia, Malaysia and Thailand.

---

2 To make the sauce, carefully remove the seeds from the chilies and chop the flesh roughly. Put the chilies and the other sauce ingredients in a food processor or blender with 3 tablespoons of the coconut milk. Process until smooth.

3 Heat a wok, then add the oil. When the oil is hot, stir-fry the seafood for 2–3 minutes, then remove.

4 Add the sauce and the remaining coconut milk to the wok, then return the seafood. Bring to a boil, season well and serve with crusty bread.

Karahi Shrimp and Fenugreek

The black-eyed peas, shrimp and paneer in this dish mean that it is rich in protein. The combination of both ground and fresh fenugreek makes the dish very fragrant and delicious.

INGREDIENTS

Serves 4–6

¼ cup corn oil
2 onions, sliced
2 medium tomatoes, sliced
1¹/₂ teaspoons minced garlic
1 teaspoon chili powder
1 teaspoon grated fresh ginger
1 teaspoon ground cumin
1 teaspoon ground coriander
1 teaspoon salt
1 cup paneer (Indian cheese), cubed
1 teaspoon ground fenugreek
1 bunch fresh fenugreek leaves
4 ounces shelled cooked shrimp
2 fresh red chilies, sliced
2 tablespoons chopped fresh cilantro
¹/₄ cup canned black-eyed peas, drained
1 tablespoon lemon juice

1 Heat the oil in a preheated wok. Lower the heat slightly and add the onions and tomatoes. Fry, stirring occasionally, for about 3 minutes.

2 Add the garlic, chili powder, ginger, ground cumin, ground coriander, salt, paneer and the ground and fresh fenugreek. Lower the heat and stir-fry for about 2 minutes.

3 Add the shrimp, red chilies, fresh cilantro and the black-eyed peas and mix well. Cook for another 3–5 minutes, stirring occasionally, until the shrimp are heated through.

4 Finally, sprinkle on the lemon juice and serve.

Paneer with Shrimp

Paneer (Indian cheese) makes an excellent substitute for red meat. In this recipe paneer is combined with jumbo shrimp to make a memorable stir-fry dish.

INGREDIENTS

Serves 4

12 cooked jumbo shrimp
6 ounces paneer (Indian cheese)
2 tablespoons tomato paste
$^1/_4$ cup plain yogurt
$1^1/_2$ teaspoons garam masala
1 teaspoon chili powder
1 teaspoon minced garlic
1 teaspoon salt
2 teaspoons mango powder
1 teaspoon ground coriander
1 stick butter
1 tablespoon corn oil
3 fresh green chilies, chopped
3 tablespoons chopped fresh cilantro
$^2/_3$ cup light cream or half-and-half

1 Shell the shrimp and cube the paneer.

2 Combine the tomato paste, yogurt, garam masala, chili powder, garlic, salt, mango powder and ground coriander in a mixing bowl and set aside.

3 Melt the butter with the oil in a wok. Lower the heat slightly and stir-fry the paneer and shrimp for about 2 minutes. Remove with a slotted spoon and drain on paper towels. Set aside.

4 Pour the spice mixture into the butter and oil left in the pan and stir-fry for about 1 minute.

5 Add the paneer and shrimp, and cook for 7–10 minutes, stirring occasionally, until the shrimp are heated through.

6 Add the fresh chilies and most of the cilantro, and pour in the cream. Heat for about 2 minutes, garnish with the remaining fresh cilantro and serve.

COOK'S TIP

To make paneer at home, bring 4 cups milk to a boil over low heat. Add 2 tablespoons lemon juice and stir constantly and gently until the milk thickens and begins to curdle. Strain the curdled milk through a strainer lined with cheesecloth. Set aside under a heavy weight for 1½–2 hours to press to a flat shape about ½ inch thick.

Make the paneer a day before you plan to use it in a recipe; then it will be firmer and easier to handle. Cut and use as required; it will keep for about 1 week in the refrigerator.

Boemboe Bali of Fish

The island of Bali has wonderful fish, surrounded as it is by the sparkling blue sea. This simple fish "curry" is packed with many of the characteristic flavors associated with Indonesia.

Ingredients

Serves 4–6

1½ pounds cod or haddock fillet
½ teaspoon shrimp paste
2 red or white onions
1 inch fresh ginger root, peeled
    and sliced
½ inch fresh *laos*, peeled and sliced, or
    1 teaspoon *laos* powder
2 garlic cloves
1–2 fresh red chilies, seeded, or
    2 teaspoons Chili Sambal, or
    1–2 teaspoons chili powder
6–8 tablespoons sunflower oil
1 tablespoon dark soy sauce
1 teaspoon tamarind pulp, soaked in
    2 tablespoons warm water
1 cup water
celery leaves or chopped fresh chili,
    to garnish
boiled rice, to serve

1 Skin the fish, remove any bones and then cut the flesh into bite-size pieces. Pat dry with paper towels and set aside.

2 Grind the shrimp paste, onions, ginger, *laos*, garlic and fresh chilies, if using, to a paste in a food processor or with a mortar and pestle. Stir in the Chili Sambal or chili powder and *laos* powder, if using.

3 Heat 2 tablespoons of the oil and fry the spice mixture, stirring, until it gives off a rich aroma. Add the soy sauce. Strain the tamarind and add the juice and water. Cook for 2–3 minutes.

----- Variation -----

Substitute 1 pound cooked large shrimp. Add them 3 minutes before the end.

4 In a separate pan, fry the fish in the remaining oil for 2–3 minutes. Turn only once so that the pieces stay whole. Lift out with a slotted spoon and put into the sauce.

5 Cook the fish in the sauce for 3 minutes more and serve with boiled rice. Garnish the dish with feathery celery leaves or a little chopped fresh chili, if liked.

Braised Whole Fish in Chili and Garlic Sauce

This is a classic Szechuan recipe. When it is served in a restaurant, the fish's head and tail are usually discarded before cooking, and used in other dishes. A whole fish may be used, however, and always looks impressive, especially for special occasions and formal dinner parties.

INGREDIENTS

Serves 4–6

1 carp, bream, sea bass, trout, grouper or gray mullet (1½ pounds), cleaned
1 tablespoon light soy sauce
1 tablespoon Chinese rice wine or dry sherry
vegetable oil, for deep-frying

For the sauce

2 garlic cloves, finely chopped
2–3 scallions, finely chopped, with the white and green parts separated
1 teaspoon finely chopped fresh ginger
2 tablespoons chili bean sauce
1 tablespoon tomato paste
2 teaspoons light brown sugar
1 tablespoon rice vinegar
½ cup chicken stock
1 tablespoon cornstarch paste
few drops of sesame oil

1 Rinse and dry the fish well. Using a sharp knife, score both sides of the fish down to the bone with diagonal cuts about 1 inch apart. Rub both sides of the fish with the soy sauce and rice wine. Set aside for 10–15 minutes to marinate.

2 Heat sufficient oil for deep-frying in a wok. When it is hot, add the fish and fry for 3–4 minutes on both sides, until golden brown.

3 To make the sauce, pour away all but about 1 tablespoon of the oil. Push the fish to one side of the wok and add the garlic, the white part of the scallions, the ginger, chili bean sauce, tomato paste, sugar, vinegar and stock. Bring to a boil and braise the fish in the sauce for 4–5 minutes, turning it over once. Add the green part of the scallions. Stir in the cornstarch paste to thicken the sauce. Sprinkle with a little sesame oil and serve.

Indian Seafood with Vegetables

The spicy seafood is cooked separately and combined with vegetables at the last minute.

INGREDIENTS

Serves 4
For the seafood
8 ounces cod, or any other firm, white fish
8 ounces shelled cooked shrimp
6 crab sticks, halved lengthwise
1 tablespoon lemon juice
1 teaspoon ground coriander
1 teaspoon chili powder
1 teaspoon salt
1 teaspoon ground cumin
¼ cup cornstarch
⅔ cup corn oil

For the vegetables
⅔ cup corn oil
2 onions, chopped
1 teaspoon onion seeds
¼ cauliflower, cut into florets
4 ounces green beans, cut into 1-inch lengths
1 cup canned corn
1 teaspoon shredded fresh ginger
1 teaspoon chili powder
1 teaspoon salt
4 fresh green chilies, sliced
2 tablespoons chopped fresh cilantro
lime slices, to garnish

1 Skin the fish and cut into small cubes. Put it in a mixing bowl with the shrimp and crab sticks.

COOK'S TIP

Raita makes a delicious accompaniment to this seafood dish. Whisk 1¼ cups plain yogurt, then whisk in ½ cup water. Stir in 1 teaspoon salt, 2 tablespoons chopped fresh cilantro and 1 finely chopped green chili. Garnish with slices of cucumber and 1 or 2 mint sprigs.

2 In a separate bowl, combine the lemon juice, ground coriander, chili powder, salt and ground cumin. Pour this over the seafood and combine thoroughly using your hands.

3 Sprinkle on the cornstarch and mix again until the seafood is well coated. Set aside in the refrigerator for about 1 hour to let the flavors develop fully.

4 To make the vegetable mixture, heat the oil in a preheated wok. Add the onions and the onion seeds and stir-fry until lightly browned.

5 Add the cauliflower, green beans, corn, ginger, chili powder, salt, green chilies and fresh cilantro. Stir-fry for 7–10 minutes over medium heat, making sure that the cauliflower florets retain their shape.

6 Spoon the fried vegetables around the edge of a shallow dish, leaving a space in the middle for the seafood, and keep warm.

7 Wash and dry the pan, then heat the oil to fry the seafood pieces. Fry the seafood pieces in two or three batches, until they turn golden brown. Remove with a slotted spoon and drain on paper towels.

8 Arrange each batch of seafood in the middle of the dish of vegetables and keep warm while you fry the remaining batches. Garnish with lime slices and serve immediately.

Braised Fish Fillet with Mushrooms

This is the Chinese stir-fried version of the French *filets de sole bonne femme* (sole cooked with mushrooms and wine sauce).

INGREDIENTS

Serves 4

1 pound lemon sole or flounder fillets
1 teaspoon salt
$^1/_2$ egg white
2 tablespoons cornstarch paste
about $2^1/_2$ cups vegetable oil
1 tablespoon finely chopped scallions
$^1/_2$ teaspoon finely chopped fresh ginger
$1^1/_2$ cups white mushrooms,
    thinly sliced
1 teaspoon light brown sugar
1 tablespoon light soy sauce
2 tablespoons Chinese rice wine or
    dry sherry
1 tablespoon brandy
about $^2/_3$ cup stock
few drops of sesame oil

1 Trim off the soft bones along the edge of the fish, but leave the skin on. Cut each fillet into bite-size pieces. Mix the fish with a little salt, the egg white and about half of the cornstarch paste.

─── COOK'S TIP ───

You could substitute straw mushrooms, so called because they are grown on beds of rice straw. They have a subtle flavor and a slightly slippery texture.

2 Heat the oil in a preheated wok until medium-hot, add the fish, slice by slice, and stir gently so the pieces do not stick. Remove after about 1 minute and drain. Pour off the excess oil, leaving about 2 tablespoons in the wok.

3 Stir-fry the scallions, ginger and mushrooms for 1 minute. Add the sugar, soy sauce, rice wine or sherry, brandy and stock. Bring to a boil. Return the fish to the wok and braise for 1 minute. Stir in the remaining cornstarch paste to thicken the sauce, sprinkle with sesame oil and serve.

Shrimp Fu-yung

This is a very colorful dish that is simple to make in a wok. Most of the preparation can be done well in advance.

INGREDIENTS

Serves 4

3 eggs
1 tablespoon finely chopped scallion
3–4 tablespoons vegetable oil
8 ounces uncooked shrimp, shelled
2 teaspoons cornstarch paste
$^1/_2$ cup green peas
1 tablespoon Chinese rice wine or
    dry sherry
salt

1 Reserving 1 teaspoon of egg white, beat the eggs with a pinch of salt and a few pieces of the scallion. Heat a little oil in a preheated wok over medium heat. Add the egg mixture and stir to scramble. Remove the scrambled eggs and reserve.

2 Mix the shrimp with a little salt, the reserved egg white and the cornstarch paste. Stir-fry the peas in hot oil for 30 seconds Add the shrimp.

3 Add the remaining scallion. Stir-fry for 1 minute, then stir the mixture into the scrambled egg with the wine or sherry and serve.

Fish Fillets in Spicy Coconut Sauce

Use fresh fish fillets to make this dish if you can, as they have much more flavor than frozen ones. However, if you are using frozen fillets, make sure that they are thawed before you begin to cook.

INGREDIENTS

Serves 4
2 tablespoons corn oil
1 teaspoon onion seeds
4 dried red chilies
3 garlic cloves, sliced
1 onion, sliced
2 tomatoes, sliced
2 tablespoons dry unsweetened coconut
1 teaspoon salt
1 teaspoon ground coriander
4 whitefish fillets, such as sole or
   flounder (each about 3 ounces)
²/₃ cup water
1 tablespoon lime juice
1 tablespoon chopped fresh cilantro
cooked rice, to serve (optional)

1 Heat the oil in a wok. Lower the heat slightly and add the onion seeds, dried red chilies, garlic slices and onion. Cook for 3–4 minutes, stirring once or twice.

2 Add the tomatoes, coconut, salt and coriander and stir thoroughly.

3 Cut each fish fillet into three pieces. Drop the fish pieces into the mixture and turn them over gently until they are well coated.

4 Cook for 5–7 minutes, lowering the heat if necessary. Add the water, lime juice and fresh cilantro and cook for another 3–5 minutes, until the water has mostly evaporated. Serve immediately with rice, if desired.

COOK'S TIP

The Indian equivalent of the Chinese wok is the karahi. It is usually round-bottomed with two carrying handles. Like the wok, the karahi is traditionally made of cast iron in order to withstand the high temperatures and hot oil used in cooking. They are now made in a variety of different metals and are available in a range of sizes, including small ones for individual servings.

Thai Fish Cakes

Bursting with flavors of chilies, lime and lemongrass, these little fish cakes make a wonderful appetizer or light lunch dish.

INGREDIENTS

Serves 4

1 pound white fish fillets, such as cod or haddock
3 scallions, sliced
2 tablespoons chopped fresh cilantro
2 tablespoons Thai red curry paste
1 fresh green chili, seeded and chopped
2 teaspoons grated lime zest
1 tablespoon lime juice
2 tablespoons peanut oil
flour, for dusting
salt
crisp lettuce leaves, shredded
   scallions, fresh red chili slices, fresh
   cilantro sprigs and lime wedges,
   to serve

1 Cut the fish into chunks, then place them in a blender or food processor.

2 Add the scallions, cilantro, red curry paste, green chili, lime zest and juice to the fish. Season with salt. Process until finely ground.

3 Using lightly floured hands, divide the mixture into 16 pieces and shape each one into a small cake about 1½ inches across. Place the fish cakes on a plate, cover with plastic wrap and chill for about 2 hours, until firm.

4 Heat a wok over high heat until hot. Add the oil and swirl it around. Fry the fish cakes, a few at a time, for 6–8 minutes, turning them over carefully until evenly browned. Drain each batch on paper towels and keep hot while you are cooking the remainder. Serve on a bed of crisp lettuce leaves with shredded scallions, red chili slices, fresh cilantro sprigs and lime wedges.

Spiced Salmon Stir-fry

Marinating the salmon allows all the flavors to develop, and the lime juice tenderizes the fish beautifully, so it needs very little stir-frying—be careful not to overcook it.

INGREDIENTS

Serves 4
4 salmon steaks (about 8 ounces each)
4 whole star anise
2 lemongrass stalks, sliced
juice of 3 limes
finely grated zest of 3 limes
2 tablespoons honey
2 tablespoons peanut oil
salt and ground black pepper
lime wedges, to garnish

1 Remove the middle bone from each steak, using a very sharp filleting knife, to make two strips from each one.

2 Remove the skin by inserting the knife at the thin end of each piece of salmon and sliding it along under the flesh. Sprinkle 1 teaspoon salt on the cutting board to prevent the fish from slipping while you do this.

3 Roughly crush the star anise in a mortar with a pestle. Place the salmon in a nonmetallic dish and add the star anise, lemongrass, lime juice and zest and honey. Season well with salt and pepper. Turn the salmon strips to coat. Cover and set in the refrigerator to marinate overnight.

4 Carefully drain the salmon, reserving the marinade, and pat dry with paper towels.

5 Heat a wok, then add the oil. When the oil is hot, add the salmon and stir-fry, stirring constantly, until cooked. Increase the heat, add the marinade and bring to a boil. Garnish with lime wedges and serve.

COOK'S TIP

Star anise contains the same oil as the more familiar Mediterranean spice anise or aniseed, but looks completely different. Its star-shaped pods are particularly attractive, so it is often used whole in Chinese cooking for its decorative effect. It is also becoming increasingly popular with Western cooks for the same reason. It is an essential ingredient in many classic Chinese recipes and is one of the spices that constitute five-spice powder. The flavor of star anise is very strong and licorice-tasting, with deeper undertones than its European counterpart.

Chunky Fish with Bell Peppers

Try to find as many different colors of peppers as possible to make this very attractive dish.

INGREDIENTS

Serves 2–4

1 pound cod or any other firm, white fish
1¹/₂ teaspoons ground cumin
2 teaspoons mango powder
1 teaspoon ground coriander
¹/₂ teaspoon chili powder
1 teaspoon salt
1 teaspoon grated fresh ginger
3 tablespoons cornstarch
²/₃ cup corn oil
1 each green, yellow and red bell peppers, seeded and chopped
8–10 cherry tomatoes, to garnish

1 Skin the fish, then cut it into small cubes. Put the cubes in a large mixing bowl and add the ground cumin, mango powder, ground coriander, chili powder, salt, ginger and cornstarch. Combine thoroughly until the fish is well coated.

2 Heat the oil in a wok. When it is hot, lower the heat slightly and add the fish pieces, three or four at a time. Fry for about 3 minutes, turning them and stirring constantly.

3 Drain the fish pieces on paper towels and transfer them to a serving dish. Keep them warm while you fry the remaining fish pieces.

4 Fry the peppers in the remaining oil for about 2 minutes. They should still be slightly crisp. Drain on paper towels.

5 Add the cooked peppers to the fish on the serving dish and garnish with the cherry tomatoes.

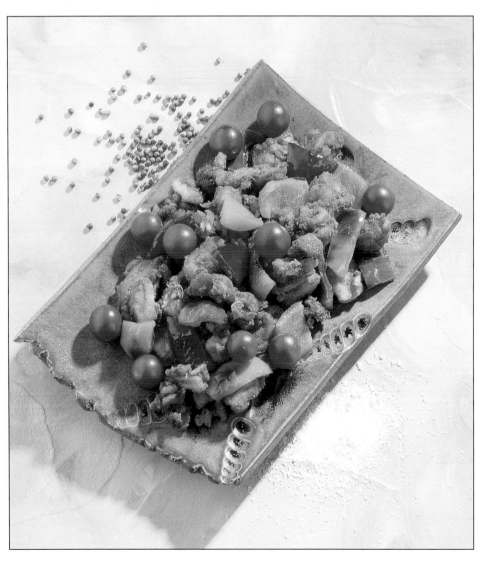

COOK'S TIP

This dish is delicious when served with raita and paratha, a traditional Indian unleavened bread with rich flaky layers.

Sweet and Sour Fish

When fish is cooked in this way the skin becomes crispy on the outside, while the flesh remains moist and juicy inside. The sweet and sour sauce, with its colorful cherry tomatoes, complements the fish beautifully.

INGREDIENTS

Serves 4–6

1 large or 2 medium-size fish such as
   snapper or mullet, heads removed
2 tablespoons cornstarch
½ cup vegetable oil
1 tablespoon chopped garlic
1 tablespoon chopped fresh ginger
2 tablespoons chopped shallots
8 ounces cherry tomatoes
2 tablespoons red wine vinegar
2 tablespoons sugar
2 tablespoons tomato ketchup
1 tablespoon fish sauce
3 tablespoons water
salt and freshly ground black pepper
cilantro leaves and shredded scallions,
   to garnish

1 Thoroughly rinse and clean the fish. Score the skin diagonally on both sides of the fish.

2 Coat the fish lightly on both sides with 1 tablespoon cornstarch. Shake off any excess.

3 Heat the oil in a wok or large frying pan and slide the fish into the wok. Reduce the heat to medium and fry the fish for about 6–7 minutes, until crisp and brown on both sides.

4 Remove the fish with a spatula and place on a large platter.

5 Pour off all but 2 tablespoons of the oil and add the garlic, ginger and shallots. Fry until golden.

6 Add the cherry tomatoes and cook until they burst open. Stir in the vinegar, sugar, tomato ketchup and fish sauce. Simmer gently for 1–2 minutes and adjust the seasoning to taste.

7 Blend the remaining 1 tablespoon cornstarch with the water. Stir into the sauce and heat until it thickens. Pour the sauce over the fish and garnish with cilantro leaves and shredded scallions.

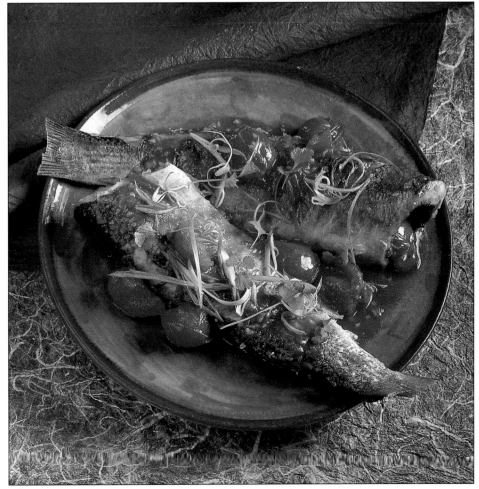

Malaysian Fish Curry

Fish cooked in a wok full of coconut milk makes a mouthwatering curry.

INGREDIENTS

Serves 4–6

$1^1/_2$ pounds monkfish or red snapper fillet

3 tablespoons grated or dry unsweetened coconut

2 tablespoons vegetable oil

1-inch piece galangal or fresh ginger, peeled and thinly sliced

2 small red chilies, seeded and finely chopped

2 garlic cloves, crushed

2-inch piece lemongrass, shredded

1 piece shrimp paste ($1/_2$ inch square), or 1 tablespoon fish sauce

14-ounce can coconut milk

$2^1/_2$ cups chicken stock

$1/_2$ teaspoon ground turmeric

1 tablespoon sugar

juice of 1 lime or $1/_2$ lemon

salt

cilantro and lime slices, to garnish

1 Cut the fish into large chunks, season with salt and set aside.

2 Dry-fry the coconut in a large wok until evenly brown. Add the oil, galangal or ginger, chilies, garlic and lemongrass and fry briefly. Stir in the shrimp paste. Strain the coconut milk through a strainer, reserving what remains in the strainer, then add to the wok.

COOK'S TIP

Sambal, a fiery hot relish, is traditionally served with this curry. Combine 2 skinned and chopped tomatoes, 1 finely chopped onion, 1 finely chopped green chili and 2 tablespoons lime juice. Season to taste with salt and pepper and sprinkle with 2 tablespoons grated coconut.

---

3 Add the chicken stock, turmeric, sugar, a little salt and the lime or lemon juice. Simmer for 10 minutes. Add the fish and simmer for 6–8 minutes. Stir in the reserved part of the coconut milk and simmer to thicken. Garnish with cilantro and lime slices and serve.

Vinegar Fish

Fish cooked in a spicy mixture that includes chilies, ginger and vinegar is an Indonesian specialty. It is a method that lends itself particularly well to strong-flavored, oily fish, such as the mackerel used here.

INGREDIENTS

Serves 2–3

2–3 medium mackerel, filleted
2–3 fresh red chilies, seeded
4 macadamia nuts or 8 almonds
1 red onion, quartered
2 garlic cloves, crushed
½-inch piece fresh ginger, peeled and sliced
1 teaspoon ground turmeric
3 tablespoons vegetable oil
3 tablespoons wine vinegar
⅔ cup water
salt
deep-fried onions and finely chopped fresh chili, to garnish
plain cooked rice or coconut rice, to serve (optional)

1 Rinse the mackerel fillets in cold water and dry well on paper towels. Set aside.

COOK'S TIP

To make coconut rice, put ⅔ cup washed long-grain rice in a heavy saucepan with ½ teaspoon salt, a 2-inch piece of lemongrass and 1 ounce creamed coconut. Add 3 cups boiling water and stir once to prevent the grains from sticking together. Simmer over medium heat for 10–12 minutes. Remove the pan from the heat, cover and set aside for 5 minutes. Fluff the rice with a fork or chopsticks before serving.

2 Put the chilies, macadamia nuts or almonds, onion, garlic, ginger, turmeric and 1 tablespoon of the oil in a food processor and process to form a paste. Alternatively, pound them together in a mortar with a pestle to form a paste. Heat the remaining oil in a wok. When it is hot, add the paste and cook for 1–2 minutes without browning. Stir in the vinegar and water and season with salt to taste. Bring to a boil, then lower the heat.

3 Add the mackerel fillets to the sauce and simmer for 6–8 minutes, or until the fish is tender and cooked.

4 Transfer the fish to a warm serving dish. Bring the sauce to a boil and cook for 1 minute or until it has reduced slightly. Pour the sauce over the fish, garnish with deep-fried onions and chopped chili and serve with rice, if desired.

Fragrant Swordfish with Ginger and Lemongrass

Swordfish is a firm-textured, meaty fish that cooks well in a wok if it has been marinated as steaks rather than cut strips. It can be a little dry, but this is counteracted by the marinade. If you cannot get swordfish, use any variety of fresh tuna.

INGREDIENTS

Serves 4

1 kaffir lime leaf
3 tablespoons rock salt
5 tablespoons light brown sugar
4 swordfish steaks (about 8 ounces each)
1 lemongrass stalk, sliced
1-inch piece fresh ginger, cut into matchsticks
1 lime
1 tablespoon peanut oil
1 large ripe avocado, peeled and pitted
salt and ground black pepper

1 Bruise the lime leaf by crushing slightly, to release the flavor.

COOK'S TIP

Kaffir lime leaves are intensely aromatic, with a distinctive figure-eight shape. They are used extensively in Indonesian and Thai cooking. Thai cuisine also makes use of the rind of the lime from this tree.

2 To make the marinade, process the rock salt, brown sugar and lime leaf in a food processor or blender until thoroughly blended.

3 Place the swordfish steaks in a bowl. Sprinkle the marinade over them and add the lemongrass and ginger matchsticks. Set aside in the refrigerator for 3–4 hours to marinate.

4 Rinse off the marinade and pat the fish dry with paper towels.

5 Peel the lime. Remove any excess pith from the peel. Cut the peel into very thin strips. Squeeze the juice from the fruit.

6 Heat a wok, then add the oil. When the oil is hot, add the lime rind and then the swordfish steaks. Stir-fry for 3–4 minutes. Add the lime juice. Remove the wok from the heat. Slice the avocado and add to the fish. Season to taste and serve.

Green Shrimp Curry

A popular, fragrant, creamy curry that takes very little time to prepare. It can also be made with thin strips of chicken meat.

INGREDIENTS

Serves 4–6

2 tablespoons vegetable oil
2 tablespoons green curry paste
1 pound jumbo shrimp, shelled
   and deveined
4 kaffir lime leaves, torn
1 lemongrass stalk, bruised
   and chopped
1 cup unsweetened coconut milk
2 tablespoons fish sauce
½ cucumber, seeded and cut into
   thin batons
10–15 basil leaves
4 green chilies, sliced, to garnish

1 Heat the oil in a frying pan. Add the green curry paste and fry until bubbling and fragrant.

2 Add the shrimp, kaffir lime leaves and lemongrass. Fry for 1–2 minutes, until the shrimp are pink.

3 Stir in the coconut milk and bring to a gentle boil. Simmer, stirring occasionally, for about 5 minutes or until the shrimp are tender.

4 Stir in the fish sauce, cucumber and basil, then top with the sliced green chilies and serve.

Stir-fried Shrimp with Broccoli

This is a very colorful dish, highly nutritious and at the same time extremely delicious; furthermore, it is neither time-consuming nor difficult to prepare.

INGREDIENTS

Serves 4

6–8 ounces uncooked shrimp, shelled and deveined
1 teaspoon salt
1 tablespoon Chinese rice wine or dry sherry
1 tablespoon egg white
1 tablespoon cornstarch paste
8 ounces broccoli
about 1¼ cups vegetable oil
1 scallion, cut into short sections
1 teaspoon light brown sugar
about 2 tablespoons light fish stock or water
1 teaspoon light soy sauce
few drops of sesame oil

1 Cut each shrimp in half lengthwise. Mix with a pinch of salt and about 1 teaspoon of the wine or sherry, the egg white and cornstarch paste.

2 Cut the broccoli into florets; remove the rough skin from the stalks, then cut the stalks into even-size pieces.

3 Heat the oil in a preheated wok and stir-fry the shrimp for about 30 seconds. Remove with a slotted spoon and drain thoroughly.

4 Pour off the excess oil, leaving 2 tablespoons in the wok. Add the broccoli and scallion, stir-fry for about 2 minutes, then add the remaining salt and the sugar, followed by the shrimp and stock or water. Add the soy sauce and remaining wine or sherry. Blend well, then add the sesame oil and serve.

Chili Crabs

It is possible to find variations on *kepitang pedas* all over Asia. It will be memorable whether you eat it in simple surroundings or in an elegant restaurant.

Ingredients

Serves 4

2 cooked crabs (about 1½ pounds)
½ teaspoon shrimp paste
2 garlic cloves
2 fresh red chilies, seeded, or 1 teaspoon
  chopped chili from a jar
½ inch fresh ginger, peeled and sliced
4 tablespoons sunflower oil
1¼ cups tomato ketchup
1 tablespoon dark brown sugar
½ cup warm water
4 scallions, chopped, to garnish
cucumber chunks and hot toast,
  to serve (optional)

1 Remove the large claws of one crab and turn onto its back with the head facing away from you. Use your thumbs to push the body up from the main shell. Discard the stomach sac and "dead men's fingers," i.e. lungs and any green matter. Leave the creamy brown meat in the shell and cut the shell in half with a cleaver or heavy knife. Cut the body section in half and crack the claws with a sharp blow from a hammer or cleaver. Avoid splintering the claws. Repeat with the other crab.

2 Grind the shrimp paste, garlic, chilies and ginger in a food processor or with a mortar and pestle.

3 Heat a wok and add the oil. Fry the spice paste, stirring it constantly, without browning.

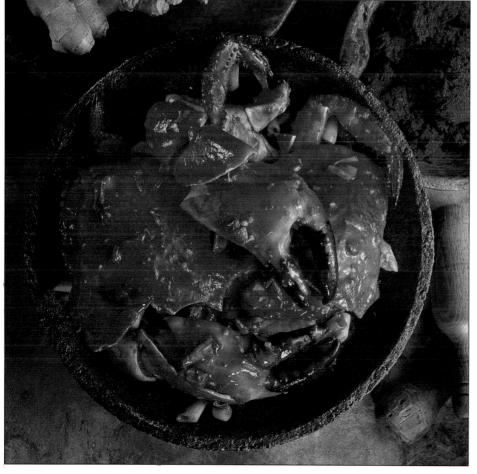

4 Stir in the tomato ketchup, sugar and water and mix the sauce well. When just boiling, add all the crab pieces and toss in the sauce until well-coated and hot. Serve in a large bowl, sprinkled with the scallions. Place in the center of the table for everyone to help themselves. Accompany this finger-licking dish with cool cucumber chunks and hot toast for mopping up the sauce, if you like.

Stir-fried Shrimp with Tamarind

The sour, tangy flavor that is characteristic of many Thai dishes comes from tamarind. Fresh tamarind pods, from the tamarind tree, can sometimes be bought, but preparing them for cooking is a laborious process. The Thais prefer to use compressed blocks of tamarind paste, which is simply soaked in warm water and then strained.

INGREDIENTS

Serves 4–6
2 tablespoons tamarind paste
²/₃ cup boiling water
2 tablespoons vegetable oil
2 tablespoons chopped onion
2 tablespoons palm sugar
2 tablespoons chicken stock or water
1 tablespoon fish sauce
6 dried red chilies, fried
1 pound uncooked shelled shrimp
1 tablespoon fried chopped garlic
2 tablespoons fried sliced shallots
2 scallions, chopped, to garnish

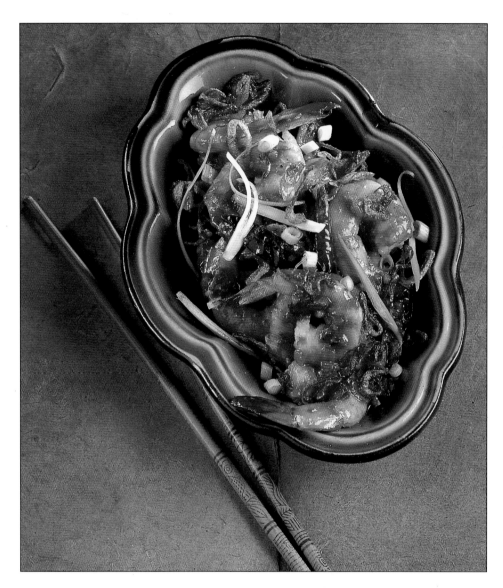

1 Put the tamarind paste in a small bowl, pour over the boiling water and stir well to break up any lumps. Set aside for 30 minutes. Strain, pushing as much of the juice through as possible. Measure 6 tablespoons of the juice, which is the amount needed, and store the rest in the fridge. Heat the oil in a wok. Add the chopped onion and fry until golden brown.

2 Add the sugar, stock, fish sauce, dried chilies and the tamarind juice, stirring well until the sugar dissolves. Bring to a boil.

3 Add the shrimp, garlic and shallots. Stir-fry for about 3–4 minutes until the shrimp are cooked. Garnish with the chopped scallions.

Shrimp Satay

Serve this enticing and tasty dish with greens and jasmine rice.

Ingredients

Serves 4–6

1 pound jumbo shrimp, shelled, tail
   ends left intact and deveined
½ bunch cilantro leaves, to garnish
4 red chilies, finely sliced and scallions,
   cut diagonally, to garnish

For the peanut sauce

3 tablespoons vegetable oil
1 tablespoon chopped garlic
1 small onion, chopped
3–4 red chilies, crushed and chopped
3 kaffir lime leaves, torn
1 lemongrass stalk, bruised
   and chopped
1 teaspoon medium curry paste
1 cup unsweetened coconut milk
½-inch cinnamon stick
⅓ cup crunchy peanut butter
3 tablespoons tamarind juice
2 tablespoons fish sauce
2 tablespoons palm sugar
juice of ½ lemon

1 To make the sauce, heat half the oil in a wok or large frying pan and add the garlic and onion. Cook for about 3–4 minutes, until it softens.

2 Add the chilies, kaffir lime leaves, lemongrass and curry paste. Cook for a further 2–3 minutes.

Cook's Tip

Curry paste has a far superior, authentic flavor to powdered varieties. Once opened, it should be kept in the fridge and used within two months.

3 Stir in the coconut milk, cinnamon stick, peanut butter, tamarind juice, fish sauce, palm sugar and lemon juice.

4 Reduce the heat and simmer gently for 15–20 minutes until the sauce thickens, stirring occasionally to make sure that the sauce doesn't stick to the bottom of the pan.

5 Heat the rest of the oil in a wok or large frying pan. Add the shrimp and stir-fry for about 3–4 minutes, or until the shrimp turn pink and are slightly firm to the touch.

6 Mix the shrimp with the sauce. Serve garnished with cilantro leaves, red chilies and scallions.

Spiced Shrimp with Coconut

This spicy dish is based on the traditional Indonesian dish *sambal goreng udang*. Sambals are pungent, very hot dishes popular throughout southern India and Southeast Asia.

INGREDIENTS

Serves 3–4

2–3 fresh red chilies, chopped
3 shallots, chopped
1 lemongrass stalk, chopped
2 garlic cloves, chopped
thin sliver of dried shrimp paste
½ teaspoon ground galangal
1 teaspoon ground turmeric
1 teaspoon ground coriander
1 tablespoon peanut oil
1 cup water
2 kaffir lime leaves
1 teaspoon light brown sugar
2 tomatoes, skinned, seeded and
    chopped
1 cup coconut milk
1½ pounds uncooked jumbo shrimp,
    shelled and deveined
squeeze of lemon juice
salt
shredded scallions and grated
    unsweetened coconut, to garnish

1 In a mortar, pound together the chilies, shallots, lemongrass, garlic, shrimp paste, galangal, turmeric and coriander with a pestle until the mixture forms a paste.

2 Heat a wok, add the oil and swirl it around. Add the spice paste and stir-fry for 2 minutes. Pour in the water and add the kaffir lime leaves, sugar and tomatoes. Simmer for 8–10 minutes, until most of the liquid has evaporated.

— COOK'S TIP —

Dried shrimp paste, widely used in Southeast Asian cooking, is available at Asian food stores.

3 Add the coconut milk and shrimp and cook gently, stirring, for 4 minutes, until the shrimp are pink. Season with lemon juice and salt to taste. Transfer the mixture to a warm serving dish, garnish with the scallions and grated coconut, and serve.

Scallops with Ginger Relish

Buy scallops in their shells to be absolutely sure of their freshness; your fishmonger will open them for you if you find this difficult. Remember to ask for the shells, which make excellent and attractive serving dishes. Queen scallops are particularly prized for their delicate-tasting coral, or roe.

INGREDIENTS

Serves 4
8 king or queen scallops
4 whole star anise
2 tablespoons unsalted butter
salt and ground white pepper
fresh chervil sprigs and whole star
    anise, to garnish

For the relish
$^1/_2$ cucumber, peeled
salt, for sprinkling
2-inch piece fresh ginger, peeled
2 teaspoons superfine sugar
3 tablespoons rice wine vinegar
2 teaspoons ginger syrup, strained from
    a jar of preserved ginger
sesame seeds, to garnish

1 To make the relish, halve the cucumber lengthwise, scoop out the seeds with a teaspoon and discard.

2 Cut the cucumber into 1-inch pieces, place in a colander and sprinkle liberally with salt. Set aside for 30 minutes.

3 Open the scallop shells, detach the scallops and remove the edible parts. Cut each scallop into two or three slices and reserve the coral. Coarsely grind the star anise in a mortar with a pestle.

4 Place the scallop slices and coral in a bowl, sprinkle the star anise on top and season with salt and pepper. Set aside to marinate for about 1 hour.

5 Rinse the cucumber under cold water, drain well and pat dry with paper towels. Cut the ginger into thin julienne strips and mix with the cucumber, sugar, vinegar and ginger syrup. Cover and chill until needed.

6 Heat a wok and add the butter. When the butter is hot, add the scallop slices and coral and stir-fry for 2–3 minutes. Garnish with sprigs of chervil and whole star anise, and serve with the cucumber relish, sprinkled with sesame seeds.

COOK'S TIP

To prepare scallops, hold flat side up and insert a strong knife between the shells to cut through the muscle. Separate the two shells. Slide the knife blade underneath the scallop in the bottom shell to cut the second muscle. Remove the scallop and separate the edible parts—the white muscle and orange coral, or roe. The skirt can be used for making fish stock, but the other parts should be discarded.

MEAT

Pork, beef and lamb are all superb when stir-fried, but using tender cuts and making sure the meat is cut into even-size strips or cubes are the keys to success. Most of the recipes here include a delicious selection of vegetables cooked together with the meat in the same wok, so the only extras you need to prepare are some rice, a salad or, perhaps, freshly baked naan. Recipes range from the exotic Stir-fried Pork with Lychees to the hot and spicy Chili Beef with Basil, and from the delicately flavored Glazed Lamb to Fragrant Thai Meatballs.

Lemongrass Pork

Chilies and lemongrass flavor this simple stir-fry, while peanuts add crunch.

INGREDIENTS

Serves 4

1½ pounds boneless loin of pork
2 lemongrass stalks, finely chopped
4 scallions, thinly sliced
1 teaspoon salt
12 black peppercorns, coarsely crushed
2 tablespoons peanut oil
2 garlic cloves, chopped
2 fresh red chilies, seeded and chopped
1 teaspoon light brown sugar
2 tablespoons fish sauce, or to taste
¼ cup roasted unsalted peanuts, chopped
salt and ground black pepper
fresh cilantro leaves, to garnish
rice noodles, to serve

1 Trim any excess fat from the pork. Cut the meat across into ¼-inch thick slices, then cut each slice into ¼-inch strips. Put the pork into a bowl with the lemongrass, scallions, salt and crushed peppercorns. Mix well, then cover and let marinate for 30 minutes.

2 Heat a wok until hot, add the oil and swirl it around. Add the pork mixture and stir-fry for 3 minutes.

3 Add the garlic and chilies and stir-fry for another 5–8 minutes over medium heat, until the pork no longer looks pink.

4 Add the sugar, fish sauce and chopped peanuts and toss to mix. Taste and adjust the seasoning, if necessary. Serve immediately, garnished with roughly torn cilantro leaves, on a bed of rice noodles.

Stir-fried Pork with Lychees

Crispy pieces of pork with fleshy lychees make an unusual stir-fry that is ideal for a dinner party.

INGREDIENTS

Serves 4

1 pound fatty pork, such as pork belly
2 tablespoons hoisin sauce
4 scallions, sliced
6 heavy lychees, peeled, pitted and cut into slivers
salt and ground black pepper
lychees and fresh parsley sprigs, to garnish

1 Using a cleaver or sharp knife, cut the pork into bite-sized pieces.

2 Pour the hoisin sauce over the pork and marinate for 30 minutes.

3 Heat a wok, then add the pork and stir-fry for 5 minutes, until crisp and golden. Add the scallions and stir-fry for another 2 minutes.

4 Scatter the lychee slivers over the pork, and season well with salt and pepper. Garnish with fresh lychees and parsley, and serve.

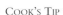

—— COOK'S TIP ——

If you cannot buy fresh lychees, this dish can be made with drained canned lychees.

Savory Pork Ribs with Snake Beans

This is a rich and pungent dish. If snake beans are hard to find, you can substitute fine green beans or wax beans.

INGREDIENTS

Serves 4–6

1½ pounds pork spare ribs or boneless pork loin
2 tablespoons vegetable oil
½ cup water
1 tablespoon palm sugar
1 tablespoon fish sauce
5 ounces snake beans, cut into 2-inch lengths
2 kaffir lime leaves, finely sliced
2 red chilies, finely sliced, to garnish

For the chili paste
3 dried red chilies, seeded and soaked
4 shallots, chopped
4 garlic cloves, chopped
1 teaspoon chopped galangal
1 lemongrass stalk, chopped
6 black peppercorns
1 teaspoon shrimp paste
2 tablespoons dried shrimp, rinsed

1 Put all the ingredients for the chili paste in a mortar and grind together with a pestle until it forms a thick paste.

2 Slice and chop the spare ribs (or pork loin) into 1½-inch lengths.

3 Heat the oil in a wok or frying pan. Add the pork and fry for about 5 minutes, until lightly browned.

4 Stir in the chili paste and continue to cook for another 5 minutes, stirring constantly to keep the paste from sticking to the pan.

5 Add the water, cover and simmer for 7–10 minutes, or until the spare ribs are tender. Season with palm sugar and fish sauce.

6 Mix in the snake beans and kaffir lime leaves and fry until the beans are cooked. Serve garnished with sliced red chilies.

Spicy Meatballs

Serve *Pergedel Djawa* with either a *sambal* or spicy sauce.

INGREDIENTS

Makes 21

1 large onion, roughly chopped
1–2 fresh red chilies, seeded
  and chopped
2 garlic cloves, crushed
¼ teaspoon shrimp paste, prepared
1 tablespoon coriander seeds
1 teaspoon cumin seeds
1 pound lean ground beef
2 teaspoons dark soy sauce
1 teaspoon dark brown sugar
juice of ½ lemon
a little beaten egg
oil for shallow-frying
salt and freshly ground black pepper
fresh cilantro sprigs, to garnish

1 Put the onion, chilies, garlic and shrimp paste in a food processor. Process but do not over-chop or the onion will become too wet and spoil the consistency of the meatballs. Dry-fry the coriander and cumin seeds in a preheated pan for about 1 minute, to release the aroma. Do not brown. Grind with a mortar and pestle.

2 Put the meat in a large bowl. Stir in the onion mixture. Add the ground coriander and cumin, soy sauce, seasoning, sugar and lemon juice. Bind with a little beaten egg and shape into small, even-size balls.

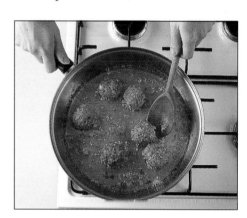

3 Chill the meatballs briefly to firm them, if necessary. Fry in shallow oil, turning often, until cooked through and browned. This will take 4–5 minutes, depending on their size.

4 Remove from the pan, drain on paper towels and serve, garnished with cilantro sprigs.

Asian Beef

This sumptuous stir-fried beef melts in the mouth, and is perfectly complemented by the delicious crunchy relish.

INGREDIENTS

Serves 4

1 pound sirloin steak
1 tablespoon sunflower oil
4 whole radishes, to garnish

For the marinade
2 garlic cloves, crushed
¼ cup dark soy sauce
2 tablespoons dry sherry
2 teaspoons dark brown sugar

For the relish
6 radishes
4-inch piece cucumber
1-inch piece preserved ginger

1 Cut the beef into thin strips. Place in a bowl.

2 To make the marinade, combine the garlic, soy sauce, sherry and sugar in another bowl. Pour it over the beef and let marinate overnight in the refrigerator.

COOK'S TIP

Dark soy sauce has a stronger, more robust flavour than light soy sauce. It is particularly useful for imparting a rich, dark colour to meat dishes.

3 To make the relish, chop the radishes and cucumber into short matchsticks, then cut the ginger into small matchsticks. Combine thoroughly in a bowl.

4 Heat a wok, then add the oil. When the oil is hot, add the meat and the marinade and stir-fry for 3–4 minutes. Serve with the relish, and garnish with a whole radish on each plate.

Pork with Eggs and Mushrooms

Traditionally, this stir-fried dish is served as a filling wrapped in thin pancakes, but it can also be served on its own with plain rice.

INGREDIENTS

Serves 4

½ cup dried Chinese mushrooms
6–8 ounces pork fillet
1 head bok choy
½ cup drained bamboo shoots
2 scallions
3 eggs
1 teaspoon salt
¼ cup vegetable oil
1 tablespoon light soy sauce
1 tablespoon Chinese rice wine or
   dry sherry
few drops of sesame oil

1 Rinse the mushrooms thoroughly in cold water and then soak in warm water for 30 minutes. Rinse thoroughly again and discard the hard stalks, if any. Dry the mushrooms and shred thinly.

2 Cut the pork fillet into matchstick-size shreds and set to one side. Thinly shred the bok choy, bamboo shoots and scallions.

3 Beat the eggs with a pinch of salt. Heat a little oil in a wok, add the eggs and lightly scramble, but do not make too dry. Remove from the wok.

4 Heat the remaining oil in the wok and stir-fry the pork for about 1 minute or until the color changes.

5 Add the vegetables to the wok and stir-fry for 1 minute. Add the remaining salt, the soy sauce and wine or sherry. Stir for 1 more minute before adding the scrambled eggs. Break up the eggs and blend well. Sprinkle with sesame oil and serve.

COOK'S TIP

Chinese fungi grow on trees and are valued more for their unusual texture than their flavor—often they have very little flavor at all. Wood ears are the most frequently used in authentic Chinese cooking, especially in stir-fries with meat or fish. They are available dried at Asian food stores and should be well rinsed, then soaked in warm water for 30 minutes and rinsed again before use. Other types of dried mushrooms and fungi are also available at Asian stores.

Chili Beef with Basil

This is a dish for chili lovers! It is very easy to prepare—all you need is a wok.

INGREDIENTS

Serves 2

about 6 tablespoons peanut oil
16–20 large fresh whole basil leaves
10 ounces sirloin steak
2 tablespoons fish sauce
1 teaspoon dark brown sugar
1–2 fresh red chilies, sliced into rings
3 garlic cloves, chopped
1 teaspoon chopped fresh ginger
1 shallot, thinly sliced
2 tablespoons finely chopped fresh basil
squeeze of lemon juice
salt and ground black pepper
Thai jasmine rice, to serve
  (see index)

1 Heat the oil in a wok and, when hot, add the whole basil leaves and fry for about 1 minute, until crisp and golden. Drain on paper towels. Remove the wok from the heat and pour off all but 2 tablespoons of the oil.

COOK'S TIP

Although not as familiar to Western cooks, Thai fish sauce is as widely used in Thai cooking as soy sauce is in Chinese cuisine. In fact, they are not dissimilar in appearance and taste. Called *nam pla*, Thai fish sauce is available at Asian food stores and some supermarkets, but if you cannot get it, soy sauce is an adequate substitute.

2 Cut the steak across the grain into thin strips. Combine the fish sauce and sugar in a bowl. Add the beef, mix well, then let marinate for about 30 minutes.

3 Reheat the oil until hot, add the chilies, garlic, ginger and shallot and stir-fry for 30 seconds. Add the beef and chopped basil, then stir-fry for about 3 minutes. Flavor with lemon juice and salt and pepper to taste.

4 Transfer to a warmed serving plate, scatter the fried whole basil leaves on top to garnish and serve immediately with Thai jasmine rice.

Thai Sweet-and-sour Pork

Sweet and sour is traditionally a Chinese creation, but the Thais do it very well. This version has an altogether fresher and cleaner flavor and it makes a good one-dish meal with rice.

INGREDIENTS

Serves 4

12 ounces lean pork
2 tablespoons vegetable oil
4 garlic cloves, finely sliced
1 small red onion, sliced
2 tablespoons fish sauce
1 tablespoon sugar
1 red bell pepper, seeded and diced
½ cucumber, seeded and sliced
2 plum tomatoes, cut into wedges
4 ounces pineapple, cut into
    small chunks
freshly ground black pepper
2 scallions, cut into short lengths
cilantro leaves and shredded scallions,
    to garnish

1 Slice the pork into thin strips. Heat the oil in a wok or large frying pan.

2 Add the garlic and fry until golden, then add the pork and stir-fry for about 4–5 minutes. Add the onion.

3 Season with fish sauce, sugar and freshly ground black pepper. Stir and cook for 3–4 minutes, or until the pork is cooked.

4 Add the rest of the vegetables, the pineapple and scallions. You may need to add a few tablespoons of water. Continue to stir-fry for about another 3–4 minutes. Serve hot, garnished with cilantro leaves and scallions.

Sizzling Beef with Celery Root Straw

Crisp celery root matchsticks look like fine pieces of straw when stir-fried, and they have a mild flavor that is quite delicious.

INGREDIENTS

Serves 4

1 pound celery root
²/₃ cup vegetable oil
1 red bell pepper
6 scallions
1 pound sirloin steak
¹/₄ cup beef stock
2 tablespoons sherry vinegar
2 teaspoons Worcestershire sauce
2 teaspoons tomato paste
salt and ground black pepper

1 Peel the celery root and then cut into fine matchsticks, using a cleaver.

2 Heat a wok, then add two-thirds of the oil. When the oil is hot, fry the celery root matchsticks in batches until golden brown and crispy. Drain well on paper towels.

3 Halve, core and seed the red bell pepper, then slice each half horizontally into 1-inch lengths. Slice the scallions diagonally into 1-inch lengths.

4 Chop the beef into thin strips, across the grain of meat.

5 Heat the wok again and add the remaining oil. When the oil is hot, stir-fry the chopped red bell pepper and scallions for 2–3 minutes.

6 Add the beef strips and stir-fry for another 3–4 minutes, until browned. Add the stock, vinegar, Worcestershire sauce and tomato paste. Season to taste and serve with the celery root straw.

COOK'S TIP

Avoid buying very large celery roots, as they tend to be woody or otherwise unpleasant in texture. Since it is a rather unwieldy vegetable, celery root is easier to peel if you cut it into more or less even-size slices first. Then peel each slice individually using a very sharp knife. They need to be peeled quite thickly to obtain a neat edge. You can then easily cut the slices into thin strips.

Stir-fried Beef in Oyster Sauce

Another simple but delicious recipe. In Thailand, fresh straw mushrooms are readily available, but oyster mushrooms make a good substitute. To make the dish even more interesting, use several types of mushroom.

INGREDIENTS

Serves 4–6

1 pound round steak
2 tablespoons soy sauce
1 tablespoon cornstarch
3 tablespoons vegetable oil
1 tablespoon chopped garlic
1 tablespoon chopped fresh ginger
8 ounces mixed mushrooms, such as
    shiitake, oyster and straw
2 tablespoons oyster sauce
1 teaspoon sugar
4 scallions, cut into short lengths
freshly ground black pepper
2 red chilies, cut into strips, to garnish

1 Slice the beef, on the diagonal, into long thin strips. Mix together the soy sauce and cornstarch in a large bowl, stir in the beef and let marinate for 1–2 hours.

COOK'S TIP

Made from extracts of oysters, oyster sauce is velvety smooth and has a savory sweet and meaty taste. There are several types available; buy the best you can afford.

2 Heat half the oil in a wok or frying pan. Add the garlic and ginger and fry until fragrant. Stir in the beef. Stir to separate the strips, let them color and cook for 1–2 minutes. Remove from the pan and set aside.

3 Heat the remaining oil in the wok. Add the shiitake, oyster and straw mushrooms. Cook until tender.

4 Return the beef to the wok with the mushrooms. Add the oyster sauce, sugar and freshly ground black pepper to taste. Mix well.

5 Add the scallions and mix together well. Serve garnished with strips of red chili.

Dry-fried Shredded Beef

Dry-frying is a unique Szechuan cooking method in which the main ingredient is first stir-fried slowly over low heat until dry, then finished off quickly with a mixture of other ingredients over high heat.

INGREDIENTS

Serves 4

1 pound flank steak
1 large or 2 small carrots
2–3 celery stalks
2 tablespoons sesame oil
1 tablespoon Chinese rice wine or
   dry sherry
1 tablespoon chili bean sauce
1 tablespoon light soy sauce
1 garlic clove, finely chopped
1 teaspoon light brown sugar
2–3 scallions, finely chopped
½ teaspoon finely chopped fresh ginger
ground Szechuan pepper

1 Cut the steak into matchstick-sized strips. Thinly shred the carrots and celery sticks.

2 Heat the sesame oil in a preheated wok (it will smoke very quickly). Reduce the heat and stir-fry the beef shreds with the rice wine or sherry, until the color changes.

3 Pour off the excess liquid and reserve. Continue stirring until the meat is absolutely dry.

4 Add the chili bean sauce, soy sauce, garlic and sugar. Blend well, then add the carrot and celery shreds. Increase the heat to high and add the scallions, ginger and the reserved liquid. Continue stirring, and when all the juice has evaporated, season with Szechuan pepper and serve.

Spiced Lamb with Spinach

INGREDIENTS

Serves 3–4

3 tablespoons vegetable oil
1¼ pounds boneless lean lamb, cut into
    1-inch cubes
1 onion, chopped
3 garlic cloves, finely chopped
½-inch piece fresh ginger, finely
    chopped
6 black peppercorns
4 whole cloves
1 bay leaf
3 green cardamom pods, crushed
1 teaspoon ground cumin
1 teaspoon ground coriander
generous pinch of cayenne pepper
⅔ cup water
2 tomatoes, peeled, seeded and
    chopped
1 teaspoon salt
1 bunch fresh spinach, trimmed,
    washed and finely chopped
1 teaspoon garam masala
crisp-fried onions and fresh cilantro
    sprigs, to garnish
naan or spiced basmati rice, to serve

1 Heat a wok until hot. Add 2 tablespoons of the oil and swirl it around. When hot, stir-fry the lamb in batches until evenly browned. Remove the lamb and set aside. Add the remaining oil, onion, garlic and ginger and stir-fry for 2–3 minutes.

2 Add the peppercorns, cloves, bay leaf, cardamom pods, cumin, ground coriander and cayenne pepper. Stir-fry for 30–45 seconds. Return the lamb and add the water, tomatoes and salt and bring to a boil. Simmer, covered, over very low heat for about 1 hour, stirring occasionally, until the meat is cooked and tender.

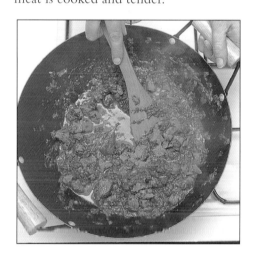

3 Increase the heat, then gradually add the spinach to the lamb, stirring to mix. Keep stirring and cooking until the spinach wilts completely and most, but not all, of the liquid has evaporated and you are left with a thick green sauce. Stir in the garam masala. Garnish with crisp-fried onions and cilantro sprigs. Serve with naan or spiced basmati rice.

Glazed Lamb

Lemon and honey make a classical stir-fry combination in sweet dishes. This lamb recipe shows how well they work together in savory dishes, too. Serve with a fresh mixed salad to complete this delicious dish.

INGREDIENTS

Serves 4

1 pound boneless lean lamb
1 tablespoon peanut oil
6 ounces snow peas, trimmed
3 scallions, sliced
2 tablespoons honey
juice of ½ lemon
2 tablespoons chopped fresh cilantro
1 tablespoon sesame seeds
salt and ground black pepper
fresh cilantro sprigs, to garnish

1 Using a cleaver, cut the lamb into thin strips.

COOK'S TIP

This recipe would work just as well made with pork or chicken instead of lamb. You could substitute chopped fresh basil for the cilantro if using chicken.

2 Heat a wok, then add the oil. When the oil is hot, stir-fry the lamb until browned all over. Remove from the wok and keep warm.

3 Add the snow peas and scallions to the hot wok and stir fry for about 30 seconds.

4 Return the lamb to the wok and add the honey, lemon juice, chopped cilantro and sesame seeds and season well. Mix thoroughly, bring to a boil, then let bubble for 1 minute, until the lamb is completely coated in the honey mixture. Serve garnished with cilantro sprigs.

Lamb Tikka

One of the best ways of tenderizing meat is to marinate it in papaya, which must be unripe or it will lend too much sweetness to what should be a savory dish. Papaya, also known as pawpaw, is readily available at most large supermarkets.

INGREDIENTS

Serves 4

1½ pounds lean lamb, cubed
1 unripe papaya
3 tablespoons plain yogurt
1 teaspoon grated fresh ginger
1 teaspoon chili powder
1 teaspoon finely chopped garlic
¼ teaspoon ground turmeric
2 teaspoons ground coriander
1 teaspoon ground cumin
2 tablespoons lemon juice
1 tablespoon chopped fresh cilantro,
    plus extra to garnish
¼ teaspoon red food coloring
1¼ cups corn oil
salt
lemon wedges and onion rings,
    to garnish
raita and naan, to serve (optional)

1 Place the cubed lamb in a large mixing bowl. Peel the papaya, cut it in half and scoop out the seeds. Cut the flesh into cubes, place in a food processor or blender and blend until it is pulped, adding about 1 tablespoon water, if necessary.

COOK'S TIP

A good-quality meat tenderizer, available at supermarkets, can be used in place of the papaya. However, the meat will need a longer marinating time and should ideally be left to tenderize overnight.

2 Pour about 2 tablespoons of the papaya pulp over the lamb cubes and rub it in well with your fingers. Set aside to marinate for at least 3 hours.

3 Meanwhile, combine the yogurt, ginger, chili powder, garlic, turmeric, coriander, cumin, lemon juice, fresh cilantro, red food coloring and 2 tablespoons of the oil. Season with salt and set aside.

4 Spoon the spicy yogurt mixture over the lamb and combine well.

5 Heat the remaining oil in a wok. When it is hot, lower the heat slightly and add the lamb cubes, a few at a time. Deep-fry the batches of lamb for 5–7 minutes or until the lamb is cooked and tender. Transfer each batch to a warmed serving dish and keep it warm while you cook the next batch.

6 When all the batches of lamb have been cooked, garnish with the lemon wedges, onion rings and fresh cilantro. Serve with raita and naan, if you wish.

Stuffed Green Bell Peppers

Stuffed bell peppers are given a different treatment here — they are deep-fried in a wok and served with a tangy sauce.

INGREDIENTS

Serves 4

8–10 ounces ground pork
4–6 water chestnuts, finely chopped
2 scallions, finely chopped
½ teaspoon finely chopped fresh ginger
1 tablespoon light soy sauce
1 tablespoon Chinese rice wine or
  dry sherry
3–4 green bell peppers
1 tablespoon cornstarch
vegetable oil, for deep-frying

For the sauce

2 teaspoons light soy sauce
1 teaspoon light brown sugar
1–2 fresh hot chilies, finely
  chopped (optional)
about 5 tablespoons stock or water

1 Combine the ground pork, water chestnuts, scallions, ginger, soy sauce and wine or sherry in a bowl.

— COOK'S TIP —

You could substitute ground beef or lamb for the ground pork used in this recipe.

---

2 Halve or quarter the bell peppers, discarding the seeds. Stuff the sections with the pork mixture and sprinkle with a little cornstarch.

3 Heat the oil in a preheated wok and deep-fry the stuffed bell peppers, with the meat sides down, for 2–3 minutes. Remove and drain.

4 Pour off the excess oil, then return the stuffed bell peppers to the wok with the meat sides up. Add the sauce ingredients, shaking the wok gently to make sure they do not stick to the bottom, and braise for 2–3 minutes. Lift the stuffed peppers on to a serving dish, meat sides up, and pour the sauce over them.

Stir-fried Pork with Vegetables

This is a basic recipe for stir-frying any meat with any vegetables, according to seasonal availability and preference.

INGREDIENTS

Serves 4

8 ounces pork loin
1 tablespoon light soy sauce
1 teaspoon light brown sugar
1 teaspoon Chinese rice wine or
   dry sherry
2 teaspoons cornstarch paste
4 ounces snow peas
1½ cups white mushrooms
1 carrot
1 scallion
¼ cup vegetable oil
1 teaspoon salt
stock (optional)
few drops of sesame oil

1 Cut the pork into thin slices, each about the size of a postage stamp. Marinate with about 1 teaspoon of the soy sauce, and the sugar, wine or sherry and cornstarch paste.

2 Trim the snow peas. Thinly slice the mushrooms. Cut the carrot into pieces roughly the same size as the pork. Cut the scallion into short sections.

3 Heat the oil in a preheated wok and stir-fry the pork for about 1 minute or until its color changes. Remove with a slotted spoon and keep warm while you cook the vegetables.

4 Add the vegetables to the wok and stir-fry for about 2 minutes. Add the salt and the partly cooked pork, and a little stock if necessary. Continue cooking and stirring for about 1 minute, then add the remaining soy sauce and blend well. Sprinkle with the sesame oil and serve.

Fragrant Thai Meatballs

INGREDIENTS

Serves 4–6

1 pound lean ground pork or beef
1 tablespoon chopped garlic
1 lemongrass stalk, finely chopped
4 scallions, finely chopped
1 tablespoon chopped fresh cilantro
2 tablespoons red curry paste
1 tablespoon lemon juice
1 tablespoon fish sauce
1 egg
rice flour for dusting
oil for frying
salt and freshly ground black pepper
sprigs of cilantro, to garnish

For the peanut sauce
1 tablespoon vegetable oil
1 tablespoon red curry paste
2 tablespoons crunchy peanut butter
1 tablespoon palm sugar
1 tablespoon lemon juice
1 cup unsweetened coconut milk

1 To make the peanut sauce, heat the oil in a small saucepan, add the curry paste and fry for 1 minute.

2 Stir in the rest of the ingredients and bring to a boil. Lower the heat and simmer for 5 minutes, until the sauce thickens.

3 To make the meatballs, combine all the ingredients except the rice flour, oil and cilantro, and season. Mix everything together thoroughly.

4 Roll and shape the meat into small balls about the size of a walnut. Dust the meatballs with rice flour.

5 Heat the oil in a wok until hot and deep fry the meatballs in batches until nicely browned and cooked through. Drain on paper towels. Serve garnished with sprigs of cilantro and accompanied by the peanut sauce.

Stuffed Thai Omelet

INGREDIENTS

Serves 4

2 tablespoons vegetable oil
2 garlic cloves, finely chopped
1 small onion, fincly chopped
8 ounces ground pork
2 tablespoons fish sauce
1 teaspoon sugar
freshly ground black pepper
2 tomatoes, peeled and chopped
1 tablespoon chopped fresh cilantro

For the omelet
5–6 eggs
1 tablespoon fish sauce
2 tablespoons vegetable oil
sprigs of cilantro and red chilies, sliced,
   to garnish

1 First heat the oil in a wok or frying pan. Add the garlic and onion and fry for 3–4 minutes, until softened. Stir in the pork and fry for about 7–10 minutes, until lightly browned.

2 Add the fish sauce, sugar, freshly ground pepper and tomatoes. Stir to combine and simmer until the sauce thickens slightly. Mix in the chopped fresh cilantro.

3 To make the omelets, whisk together the eggs and fish sauce.

4 Heat 1 tablespoon of the oil in an omelet pan or wok. Add half the beaten egg and tilt the pan to spread the egg into a thin even sheet.

5 When set, spoon half the filling over the center of the omelet. Fold in opposite sides; first the top and bottom, then the right and left sides to make a neat square package.

6 Slide out on to a warm serving dish, folded-side down. Repeat with the rest of the oil, eggs and filling. Serve garnished with sprigs of cilantro and red chilies.

POULTRY

Poultry, especially chicken, is probably the most versatile of ingredients, and this collection of palate-tingling dishes fully explores its vast range. Recipes include classics, such as Szechuan Chicken and delicious Indonesian-style Satay Chicken; family favorites, such as Sweet-and-sour Chicken and Chicken and Cashew Stir-fry; and some more unfamiliar and adventurous dishes, such as Sweet-and-sour Duck with Mango and Baby Chicken in Tamarind Sauce. From the delicately flavored and aromatic to the fiery hot and spicy, there is something here to please everyone.

Fu-yung Chicken

Because the egg whites mixed with milk are deep-fried in a wok, some imaginative cooks call this dish "Deep-fried Milk"!

INGREDIENTS

Serves 4

1 boneless chicken breast (about 6 ounces), skinned
1 teaspoon salt
4 egg whites, lightly beaten
1 tablespoon cornstarch paste
2 tablespoons milk
vegetable oil, for deep-frying
1 lettuce heart, separated into leaves
about ½ cup stock
1 tablespoon Chinese rice wine or dry sherry
1 tablespoon green peas
few drops of sesame oil
1 teaspoon diced ham, to garnish

1 Finely mince the chicken meat, then mix with a pinch of the salt, the egg whites, cornstarch paste and milk. Blend well until smooth.

2 Heat the oil in a very hot wok, but before the oil gets too hot, gently spoon the chicken and egg white mixture into the oil in batches. Do not stir, otherwise it will scatter. Stir the oil from the bottom of the wok so that the egg whites will rise to the surface. Remove as soon as the color turns bright white. Drain.

3 Pour off the excess oil, leaving about 1 tablespoon in the wok. Stir-fry the lettuce leaves with the remaining salt for 1 minute, add the stock and bring to a boil.

4 Add the chicken to the wok with the wine or sherry and peas, and blend well. Sprinkle with sesame oil, garnish with diced ham and serve.

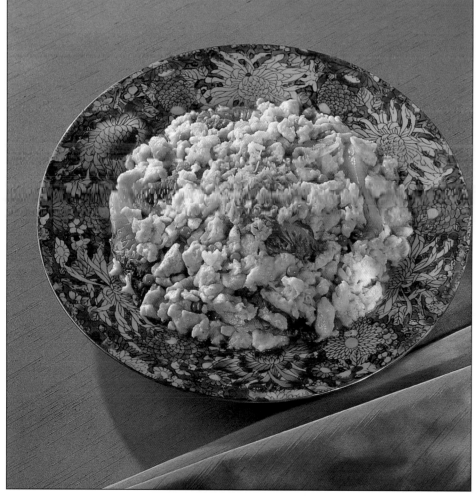

Szechuan Chicken

A wok is the ideal cooking pot for this stir-fried chicken dish. The flavors emerge wonderfully and the chicken is fresh and crisp.

INGREDIENTS

Serves 4

2 chicken thighs (about 12 ounces total), boned and skinned
$^1/_4$ teaspoon salt
$^1/_2$ egg white, lightly beaten
2 teaspoons cornstarch paste
1 green bell pepper
$^1/_4$ cup vegetable oil
3–4 dried red chilies, soaked in water for 10 minutes
1 scallion, cut into short sections
few small pieces of fresh ginger, peeled
1 tablespoon sweet bean paste or hoisin sauce
1 teaspoon chili bean paste
1 tablespoon Chinese rice wine or dry sherry
$^2/_3$ cup roasted cashews
few drops of sesame oil

1 Cut the chicken meat into small cubes, each about the size of a sugar cube. Combine the chicken, salt, egg white and cornstarch paste in a bowl.

2 Seed the bell pepper and cut it into cubes about the same size as the chicken.

3 Heat the oil in a preheated wok. Stir-fry the chicken cubes for about 1 minute or until the color changes. Remove from the wok with a slotted spoon and keep warm.

4 Add the bell pepper, chilies, scallion and ginger and stir-fry for about 1 minute. Then add the chicken, sweet bean paste, chili bean paste and wine or sherry. Blend well and cook for 1 more minute. Add the cashews and sesame oil. Serve hot.

Indonesian-style Satay Chicken

Satay traditionally forms part of a *rijsttafel* — literally, rice table — a vast feast of as many as 40 different dishes served with a large bowl of plain rice. However, for the less ambitious, creamy coconut satay makes these chicken pieces a mouthwatering dish to present at the table at any time of day.

INGREDIENTS

Serves 4

¹/₂ cup raw peanuts
3 tablespoons vegetable oil
1 small onion, finely chopped
1-inch piece fresh ginger, peeled and finely chopped
1 garlic clove, crushed
4 chicken thighs (about 1¹/₂ pounds), skinned and cut into cubes
4 ounces creamed coconut, roughly chopped
1 tablespoon chili sauce
¹/₄ cup crunchy peanut butter
1 teaspoon dark brown sugar
²/₃ cup milk
¹/₄ teaspoon salt

1 Shell the peanuts and remove the skins by rubbing them between the palms of the hands. Put them in a small bowl, add just enough water to cover and soak for 1 minute. Drain the nuts and cut them into slivers.

2 Heat the wok and add 1 teaspoon of the oil. When the oil is hot, stir-fry the peanuts for 1 minute, until crisp and golden. Remove with a slotted spoon and drain on paper towels.

3 Add the remaining oil to the hot wok. When the oil is hot, add the onion, ginger and garlic and stir-fry for 2–3 minutes, until softened but not browned. Remove with a slotted spoon and drain on paper towels.

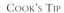

— COOK'S TIP —

Soak bamboo skewers in cold water for at least 2 hours, or preferably overnight, so that they do not char when the threaded chicken is kept warm in the oven.

4 Add the chicken pieces to the wok and stir-fry for 3–4 minutes, until crisp and golden on all sides. Thread onto presoaked bamboo skewers and keep warm.

5 Add the creamed coconut to the hot wok in small pieces and stir-fry until melted. Add the chili sauce, peanut butter and ginger mixture and simmer for 2 minutes. Stir in the sugar, milk and salt, and simmer for another 3 minutes. Serve the skewered chicken hot, with a dish of the hot dipping sauce sprinkled with the roasted peanuts.

Hot Chili Chicken

A tantalizing mixture of lemongrass and ginger provides the flavoring for this chicken feast. The ingredients are gently simmered in a wok to achieve a superb final product.

INGREDIENTS

Serves 4–6

3 chicken legs (thighs and drumsticks)
1 tablespoon vegetable oil
³/₄-inch piece fresh ginger, peeled and finely chopped
1 garlic clove, crushed
1 small red chili, seeded and finely chopped
2-inch piece lemongrass, shredded
²/₃ cup chicken stock
1 tablespoon fish sauce (optional)
2 teaspoons sugar
¹/₂ teaspoon salt
juice of ¹/₂ lemon
¹/₂ cup raw peanuts
2 scallions, shredded
rind of 1 mandarin orange or satsuma, shredded
2 tablespoons chopped fresh mint, to garnish
rice or rice noodles, to serve

1 With the heel of the knife, chop through the narrow end of the drumsticks. Remove the jointed parts of the drumsticks and thigh bones, then remove the skin.

2 Heat the oil in a large preheated wok. Add the chicken, ginger, garlic, chili and lemongrass and cook for 3–4 minutes. Add the chicken stock, fish sauce, if using, sugar, salt and lemon juice. Lower the heat, cover and simmer for 30–35 minutes.

3 To prepare the peanuts for the topping, broil or roast them under steady heat until evenly brown, 2–3 minutes. Turn the nuts out onto a dish towel and rub briskly to loosen the skins.

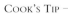

4 Serve the chicken scattered with roasted peanuts, shredded scallions and the rind of the mandarin orange. Garnish with mint and serve with rice or rice noodles.

COOK'S TIP

This dish can also be prepared using duck legs. Be sure to remove the jointed parts of the drumsticks and thigh bones to make the meat easier to eat with chopsticks.

Stir-fried Chicken with Basil and Chilies

This quick and easy chicken dish is an excellent introduction to Thai cuisine. Deep-frying the basil adds another dimension to this dish. Thai basil, which is sometimes known as Holy basil, has a unique, pungent flavor that is both spicy and sharp. The dull leaves have serrated edges.

INGREDIENTS

Serves 4–6

3 tablespoons vegetable oil
4 garlic cloves, sliced
2–4 red chilies, seeded
  and chopped
1 pound chicken, cut into
  bite-size pieces
2–3 tablespoons fish sauce
2 teaspoons dark soy sauce
1 teaspoon sugar
10–12 Thai basil leaves
2 red chilics, finely sliced and 20 Thai
  basil leaves, deep-fried (optional),
  to garnish

1 Heat the oil in a wok or large frying pan and swirl it around.

COOK'S TIP

To deep-fry Thai basil leaves, make sure that the leaves are completely dry. Deep-fry in hot oil for about 30–40 seconds, lift out and drain on paper towels.

2 Add the garlic and chilies and stir-fry until golden.

3 Add the chicken and stir-fry until it changes color.

4 Season with fish sauce, soy sauce and sugar. Continue to stir-fry for 3–4 minutes, or until the chicken is cooked. Stir in the fresh Thai basil leaves. Garnish with sliced chilies and the deep-fried basil, if using.

Chicken and Cashew Stir-fry

Hoisin sauce lends a sweet yet slightly hot note to this chicken stir-fry, while cashews add a pleasing contrast of texture.

INGREDIENTS

Serves 4

¹/₂ cup cashews
1 red bell pepper
1 pound boneless chicken breasts
3 tablespoons peanut oil
4 garlic cloves, finely chopped
2 tablespoons Chinese rice wine or dry sherry
3 tablespoons hoisin sauce
2 teaspoons sesame oil
5–6 scallions, green part only, cut into 1-inch lengths

2 Cut the red bell pepper in half and remove the seeds. Slice into thin strips. Skin the chicken fillet and cut into thin finger-length strips.

4 Add the rice wine or sherry and hoisin sauce. Continue to stir-fry until the chicken is tender and all the ingredients are evenly glazed.

1 Heat a wok until hot, add the cashews and dry-fry over low to medium heat for 1–2 minutes, until golden brown. Remove and set aside.

3 Heat the wok again until hot, add the oil and swirl it around. Add the garlic and let it sizzle in the oil for a few seconds. Add the bell pepper and chicken and stir-fry for 2 minutes.

5 Stir in the sesame oil, toasted cashews and scallions. Serve immediately.

COOK'S TIP

Use blanched almonds instead of cashews, if you prefer. For a slightly less sweet taste, you could substitute light soy sauce for the hoisin sauce.

Chicken, Ham and Broccoli Stir-fry

The charmingly poetic Chinese name for this pretty and colorful dish *jin hua yi shu ji* means "golden flower and jade tree chicken." It is a marvelous cold-buffet-style stir-fry to serve on any occasion.

INGREDIENTS

Serves 6–8
1 chicken (about 3 pounds)
2 scallions
2–3 1-inch pieces fresh ginger
1 tablespoon salt
8 ounces honey-roasted ham
1 bunch broccoli
3 tablespoons vegetable oil
1 teaspoon light brown sugar
2 teaspoons cornstarch

1 Place the chicken in a large pan and cover it with cold water. Add the scallions, ginger and about 2 teaspoons of the salt. Bring to a boil, then reduce the heat and simmer for 10–15 minutes under a tightly fitting lid. Turn off the heat and let the chicken cook itself in the hot water for at least 4–5 hours; do not lift the lid, as this will let out the residual heat.

2 Remove the chicken from the pan, reserving the liquid, and carefully cut the meat away from the bones, keeping the skin on. Slice both the chicken and ham into pieces the size of a matchbox and arrange the meats in alternating layers on a plate.

3 Cut the broccoli into small florets and stir-fry in the hot oil with the remaining salt and the sugar for 2–3 minutes. Arrange the broccoli between the rows of chicken and ham and around the edge of the plate, making a border for the meat.

4 Heat 2 tablespoons of the chicken stock and thicken it with the cornstarch. Stir until smooth, then pour it evenly all over the chicken and ham to form a thin coat of transparent jelly. Let cool before serving.

Stir-fried Sweet-and-sour Chicken

This all-in-one stir-fry has a Southeast Asian influence. It is ideal for today's cook, who is so often short of time.

INGREDIENTS

Serves 4

1 package (10 ounces) Chinese egg
 noodles
2 tablespoons vegetable oil
3 scallions, chopped
1 garlic clove, crushed
1-inch piece fresh ginger, peeled and
 grated
1 teaspoon hot paprika
1 teaspoon ground coriander
3 chicken breasts, boned and sliced
4 ounces sugar-snap peas, trimmed
1 cup baby corn, halved
1½ cups bean sprouts
1 tablespoon cornstarch
3 tablespoons soy sauce
3 tablespoons lemon juice
1 tablespoon sugar
salt
3 tablespoons chopped fresh cilantro or
 scallion tops, to garnish

1 Bring a large saucepan of salted water to a boil. Add the noodles and cook according to the package instructions if using dried noodles. If using fresh egg noodles, cook for just a few minutes, stirring occasionally to separate. Drain thoroughly, cover and keep warm.

2 Heat the oil in a preheated wok. Add the scallions and cook over gentle heat. Mix in the garlic, ginger, paprika, coriander and chicken, then stir-fry for 3–4 minutes.

3 Add the peas, baby corn and bean sprouts, cover and cook briefly. Add the noodles.

4 Combine the cornstarch, soy sauce, lemon juice and sugar in a small bowl. Add to the wok and simmer briefly to thicken. Serve immediately, garnished with chopped cilantro or scallion tops.

COOK'S TIP

Large wok lids are cumbersome and can be difficult to store in a small kitchen. Instead of using a lid, you can set a circle of waxed paper against the food surface to keep the cooking juices in.

Indian Chicken with Lentils

This is rather an unusual combination of flavors, but it is certainly worth trying! The mango powder gives a delicious, tangy flavor to this spicy dish.

INGREDIENTS

Serves 4–6

¾ cup split yellow lentils
¼ cup corn oil
2 medium leeks, chopped
6 large dried red chilies
4 curry leaves
1 teaspoon mustard seeds
2 teaspoons mango powder
2 medium tomatoes, chopped
½ teaspoon chili powder
1 teaspoon ground coriander
1 pound boneless chicken breasts, skinned and cubed
salt
1 tablespoon chopped fresh cilantro, to garnish
paratha, to serve

1 Put the lentils in a strainer and wash carefully under plenty of cold running water.

2 Put the lentils in a saucepan and add just enough water to cover. Bring to a boil and cook for 10 minutes or until they are soft but not mushy. Drain thoroughly, transfer to a bowl and set aside.

3 Heat the oil in a preheated wok until hot. Lower the heat and add the leeks, dried red chilies, curry leaves and mustard seeds and stir-fry gently for 2–3 minutes.

4 Add the mango powder, tomatoes, chili powder, ground coriander and chicken. Season with salt and stir-fry for 7–10 minutes.

COOK'S TIP

Split yellow lentils, known as chana dhal, are available at Asian stores. However, if you cannot get them, split yellow peas are a good substitute.

5 Mix in the cooked lentils and fry for another 2 minutes or until the chicken is cooked through.

6 Garnish with fresh cilantro and serve immediately with paratha.

Aromatic Chicken from Madura

Magadip is best cooked ahead so that the flavors permeate the chicken flesh making it even more delicious. A cool cucumber salad is a good accompaniment.

INGREDIENTS

Serves 4

3–3½-pound chicken, cut in quarters, or 4 chicken quarters
1 teaspoon sugar
2 tablespoons coriander seeds
2 teaspoons cumin seeds
6 whole cloves
½ teaspoon ground nutmeg
½ teaspoon ground turmeric
1 small onion
1 inch fresh ginger root, peeled and sliced
1¼ cups chicken broth or water
salt and freshly ground black pepper
boiled rice and Deep-fried Onions, to serve

1 Cut each chicken quarter in half to obtain eight pieces. Place in a flameproof casserole, sprinkle with sugar and salt and toss together. This helps release the juices in the chicken. Use the backbone and any remaining carcass to make chicken stock for use later in the recipe, if you like.

COOK'S TIP

Add a large piece of bruised ginger and a small onion to the chicken stock to ensure a good flavor.

2 Dry-fry the coriander, cumin and whole cloves until the spices give off a good aroma. Add the nutmeg and turmeric and heat briefly. Grind in a processor or with a mortar and pestle.

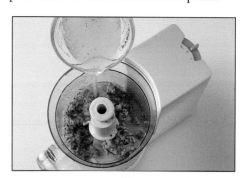

3 If using a processor, put in the onion and ginger until finely chopped. Otherwise, finely chop the onion and ginger and pound to a paste with a mortar and pestle. Add the spices and broth or water and mix well.

4 Pour over the chicken in the flameproof casserole. Cover with a lid and cook over a gentle heat until the chicken pieces are really tender, about 45–50 minutes.

5 Serve portions of the chicken, with the sauce, on boiled rice, sprinkled with crisp Deep-fried Onions.

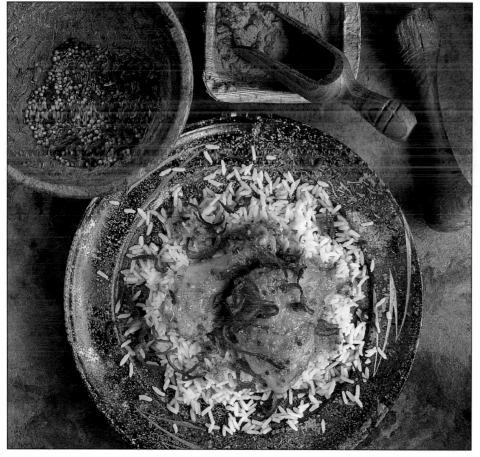

Chicken with Turmeric

INGREDIENTS

Serves 4

3–3½-pound chicken, cut in 8 pieces,
    or 4 chicken quarters, each halved
1 tablespoon sugar
3 macadamia nuts or 6 almonds
2 garlic cloves, crushed
1 large onion, quartered
1 inch fresh *laos*, peeled and sliced, or
    1 teaspoon *laos* powder
1–2 lemon grass stems, lower 2 inches
    sliced, top bruised
½ teaspoon shrimp paste
1½ inches fresh turmeric, peeled and
    sliced, or 1 tablespoon
    ground turmeric
1 tablespoon tamarind pulp, soaked in
    ⅔ cup warm water
4–6 tablespoons oil
1⅔ cup coconut milk
salt and freshly ground black pepper
Deep-fried Onions, to garnish

1 Rub the chicken joints with a little sugar and set them aside.

2 Grind the nuts and garlic in a food processor with the onion, *laos*, sliced lemon grass, shrimp paste, and turmeric. Alternatively, pound the ingredients to a paste with a mortar and pestle. Strain the tamarind pulp and reserve the juice.

3 Heat the oil in a wok and cook the paste, without browning, until it gives off a spicy aroma. Add the pieces of chicken and toss well in the spices. Add the strained tamarind juice. Spoon the coconut cream off the top of the milk and set it to one side.

4 Add the coconut milk to the pan. Cover and cook for 45 minutes, or until the chicken is tender.

5 Just before serving, stir in the coconut cream while bringing to a boil. Season and serve at once, garnished with Deep-fried Onions.

Spiced Chicken Stir-fry

INGREDIENTS

Serves 4

1 chicken (3–3½ pounds), cut in 8
    pieces
1 teaspoon each salt and ground black
    pepper
2 garlic cloves, crushed
⅝ cup sunflower oil

For the sauce
2 tablespoons butter
2 tablespoons sunflower oil
1 onion, sliced
4 garlic cloves, crushed
2 large ripe beefsteak tomatoes,
    chopped, or 14-ounce can chopped
    tomatoes with chili, drained
2½ cups water
¼ cup dark soy sauce
sliced red chili, to garnish
Deep-fried Onions, to garnish
    (optional)
boiled rice, to serve

1 Preheat the oven to 375°F. Make
two slashes in the fleshy part of
each chicken piece. Rub well with the
salt, pepper and garlic. Drizzle with a
little of the oil and bake for about
30 minutes, or shallow-fry in hot oil
for 12–15 minutes, until brown.

2 To make the sauce, heat the butter
and oil in a wok and fry the onion
and garlic until soft. Add the tomatoes,
water, soy sauce and seasoning. Boil
briskly for 5 minutes to reduce the
sauce and concentrate the flavor.

3 Add the chicken to the sauce in
the wok. Turn the chicken pieces
over in the sauce to coat them well.
Continue cooking slowly for about
20 minutes until the chicken pieces are
tender. Stir the mixture occasionally.

4 Arrange the chicken on a warm
serving platter and garnish with the
sliced chili and Deep-fried Onions, if
using. Serve with boiled rice.

Stir-fried Chicken with Pineapple

INGREDIENTS

Serves 4–6

1¼ pounds boneless chicken breasts,
    skinned and thinly sliced at an angle
2 tablespoons cornstarch
4 tablespoons sunflower oil
1 garlic clove, crushed
2-inch piece fresh ginger, peeled and
    cut in matchsticks
1 small onion, thinly sliced
1 fresh pineapple, peeled, cored and
    cubed, or 15-ounce can pineapple
    chunks in natural juice
2 tablespoons dark soy sauce or
    1 tablespoon sweet soy sauce
    (*kecap manis*)
6–8 scallions, white parts left whole,
    green tops sliced
salt and ground black pepper

1 Toss the strips of chicken in the
cornstarch with a little seasoning.
Fry in hot oil until tender.

2 Lift out of the wok or frying pan
and keep warm. Reheat the oil and
fry the garlic, ginger and onion until
soft, but not browned. Add the fresh
pineapple and ½ cup water, or the
canned pineapple pieces together with
their juice.

3 Stir in the soy sauce or *kecap manis*
and return the chicken to the pan
to heat through.

4 Taste and adjust the seasoning. Stir
in the white parts of the scallions
and half of the sliced green tops. Toss
well together and then turn the chicken
stir-fry onto a serving platter. Serve
garnished with the remaining sliced
green scallions.

Soy-braised Chicken

As the chicken is braised in the wok, so the spicy ginger sauce releases its flavor into the meat to create a succulent dish. Enjoy it hot or cold.

INGREDIENTS

Serves 6–8

1 chicken (about 3 pounds)
1 tablespoon ground Szechuan
   peppercorns
2 tablespoons grated fresh ginger
3 tablespoons light soy sauce
2 tablespoons dark soy sauce
3 tablespoons Chinese rice wine or
   dry sherry
1 tablespoon light brown sugar
vegetable oil, for deep-frying
about 2½ cups stock or water
2 teaspoons salt
2 tablespoons sugar
lettuce leaves, to serve

1 Rub the chicken inside and out with the ground pepper and fresh ginger. Marinate the chicken with the soy sauces, wine or sherry and sugar for 3 hours, turning it several times.

2 Heat the oil in a preheated wok, remove the chicken from the marinade and deep-fry for 5–6 minutes or until brown all over. Remove and drain.

COOK'S TIP

Any sauce that is left over can be stored, covered, in the refrigerator to be used again and again.

---

3 Pour off the excess oil from the wok, add the marinade with the stock, salt and sugar and bring to a boil. Return the chicken, and cover and braise in the sauce for 35–40 minutes, turning once or twice.

4 Remove the chicken from the wok and let it cool down a little before chopping it into approximately 30 bite-size pieces. Arrange on a bed of lettuce leaves, then pour some of the sauce over the chicken and serve.

Chicken with Spices and Soy Sauce

A very simple recipe, called *Ayam Kecap,* which will often appear as one of the dishes on a Padang restaurant menu. Any leftovers taste equally good when reheated the following day.

INGREDIENTS

Serves 4
3–3½-pound chicken, jointed and cut in 16 pieces
3 onions, sliced
about 4 cups water
3 garlic cloves, crushed
3–4 fresh red chilies, seeded and sliced, or 1 tablespoon chili powder
3–4 tablespoons oil
½ teaspoon ground nutmeg
6 whole cloves
1 teaspoon tamarind pulp, soaked in 3 tablespoons warm water
2–3 tablespoons dark or light soy sauce
salt
fresh red chili shreds, to garnish
boiled rice, to serve

1 Prepare the chicken and place the pieces in a large pan with one of the onions. Pour over enough water to just cover. Bring to a boil and then reduce the heat and simmer gently for 20 minutes.

2 Grind the remaining onions, with the garlic and chilies, to a fine paste in a food processor or with a mortar and pestle. Heat a little of the oil in a wok or frying pan and cook the paste to bring out the flavor, but do not allow to brown.

3 When the chicken has cooked for about 20 minutes, lift it out of the stock in the pan with a slotted spoon. Transfer the chicken to the pan with the spicy paste mixture. Toss all together over a fairly high heat so that the spices can permeate the chicken pieces. Reserve 1¼ cups of the chicken stock to add to the pan later.

4 Stir in the nutmeg and cloves. Strain the tamarind and add the tamarind juice and the soy sauce to the chicken. Cook for 2–3 minutes more, then add the reserved stock.

5 Taste and adjust the seasoning and cook, uncovered, for another 25–35 minutes, until the chicken pieces are tender.

6 Serve the chicken in a bowl, topped with shredded chili, and eat with boiled rice.

— COOK'S TIP —

Dark soy sauce is thicker and more salty than light. Adding the dark variety will give a deeper color to the chicken.

Thai Stir-fry Chicken Curry

Here chicken and potatoes are simmered in a wok filled with coconut milk, one of the essential ingredients of Thai cuisine. The end result is a superb, flavorful curry.

INGREDIENTS

Serves 4

1 onion
1 tablespoon peanut oil
1²/₃ cups coconut milk
2 tablespoons red curry paste
2 tablespoons fish sauce
1 tablespoon light brown sugar
8 ounces tiny new potatoes
1 pound boneless chicken breasts,
   skinned and cut into chunks
1 tablespoon lime juice
2 tablespoons chopped fresh mint
1 tablespoon chopped fresh basil
salt and ground black pepper
2 kaffir lime leaves, shredded, and
   1–2 fresh red chilies, seeded and
   finely shredded, to garnish

1 Cut the onion into wedges, using a sharp knife.

> ── COOK'S TIP ──
>
> You can use boneless chicken thighs instead of breasts. Simply skin them, cut the flesh into chunks and cook in the coconut milk with the potatoes.

2 Heat a wok until hot, add the oil and swirl it around. Add the onion and stir-fry for 3–4 minutes.

3 Pour in the coconut milk, then bring to a boil, stirring. Stir in the curry paste, fish sauce and sugar.

4 Add the potatoes and seasoning, cover and simmer gently for about 20 minutes.

5 Add the chicken chunks, cover and cook over low heat for another 10–15 minutes, until the chicken and potatoes are tender.

6 Stir in the lime juice, chopped mint and basil. Serve immediately, sprinkled with the shredded kaffir lime leaves and red chilies.

Khara Masala Chicken

Whole spices—*khara*—are used in this recipe, giving it a wonderfully rich flavor. This is a dry dish, so it is best served with raita and paratha.

INGREDIENTS

Serves 4

3 curry leaves
¼ teaspoon mustard seeds
¼ teaspoon fennel seeds
¼ teaspoon onion seeds
½ teaspoon crushed dried red chilies
½ teaspoon white cumin seeds
¼ teaspoon fenugreek seeds
½ teaspoon crushed pomegranate seeds
1 teaspoon salt
1 teaspoon shredded fresh ginger
3 garlic cloves, sliced
¼ cup corn oil
4 fresh green chilies, slit
1 large onion, sliced
1 medium tomato, sliced
4 chicken breasts (about 1½ pounds), skinned, boned and cubed
1 tablespoon chopped fresh cilantro, to garnish

1 Combine the curry leaves, mustard seeds, fennel seeds, onion seeds, crushed red chilies, cumin seeds, fenugreek seeds and crushed pomegranate seeds in a large bowl. Add the salt.

2 Add the shredded ginger and garlic cloves to the bowl.

3 Heat the oil in a preheated wok. When the oil is hot, add the spice mixture, then the green chilies.

4 Add the onion to the wok and stir-fry over medium heat for 5–7 minutes.

5 Add the tomato and chicken pieces to the wok and cook over medium heat for about 7 minutes or until the chicken is cooked through and the sauce has reduced slightly.

6 Stir the mixture over the heat for another 3–5 minutes, then garnish with the chopped fresh cilantro and serve immediately.

Chicken Pot

This nourishing main course combines meat with beans in a spicy sauce.

INGREDIENTS

Serves 4–6

1¼ cups dried navy beans
3 chicken legs
1 tablespoon vegetable oil
12 ounces lean pork, diced
1 chorizo, sliced (optional)
1 small carrot, peeled and
    roughly chopped
1 onion, roughly chopped
8 cups water
1 garlic clove, crushed
2 tablespoons tomato paste
1 bay leaf
2 chicken bouillon cubes
12 ounces sweet potatoes or new
    potatoes, peeled and cubed
2 teaspoons chili sauce
2 tablespoons white wine vinegar
3 firm tomatoes, skinned, seeded
    and chopped
1 head bok choy, shredded
salt and ground black pepper
3 scallions, shredded, to garnish
cooked rice, to serve

1 Put the beans in a bowl, cover with plenty of cold water and set aside to soak for 8 hours or overnight.

2 Separate the chicken drumsticks from the thighs. Chop off the narrow end of each drumstick and discard.

3 Heat the vegetable oil in a preheated wok, add the chicken, pork, sliced chorizo, if using, carrot and onion, then brown evenly

4 Drain the beans and add to the wok with the fresh water, the garlic, tomato paste and bay leaf and stir to mix. Bring to a boil, lower the heat and simmer for 2 hours, until the beans are almost tender.

5 Crumble the bouillon cubes into the wok, add the sweet or new potatoes and the chili sauce, then simmer for 15–20 minutes, until the potatoes are cooked.

6 Add the vinegar, tomatoes and bok choy to the wok, then simmer for 1–2 minutes. Season to taste with salt and pepper. Garnish with the scallions and serve with the rice.

--- COOK'S TIP ---

This dish is intended to provide enough liquid to be served as a soup for the first course, rather like a French *pot-au-feu*. This is followed by a main course of the meat and vegetables, served with rice.

Baby Chicken in Tamarind Sauce

The tamarind in this recipe gives the dish a sweet and sour flavor; this is also quite hot.

INGREDIENTS

Serves 4–6
¼ cup ketchup
1 tablespoon tamarind paste
¼ cup water
1½ teaspoons chili powder
1½ teaspoons salt
1 tablespoon sugar
1½ teaspoons grated fresh ginger
1½ teaspoons crushed garlic
2 tablespoons dry, unsweetened coconut
2 tablespoons sesame seeds
1 teaspoon poppy seeds
1 teaspoon ground cumin
1½ teaspoons ground coriander
1 baby chicken (1 pound), skinned and
    cut into 6–8 pieces
5 tablespoons corn oil
½ cup curry leaves
½ teaspoon onion seeds
3 large dried red chilies
½ teaspoon fenugreek seeds
10–12 cherry tomatoes
3 tablespoons chopped fresh cilantro
2 fresh green chilies, chopped

1 Put the ketchup, tamarind paste and water in a large mixing bowl and blend with a fork.

2 Add the chili powder, salt, sugar, ginger, garlic, coconut, sesame seeds, poppy seeds, ground cumin and ground coriander to the mixture.

3 Add the chicken pieces to the bowl and stir until they are well coated with the spice mixture. Set aside.

4 Heat the oil in a preheated wok. When it is hot, add the curry leaves, onion seeds, dried red chilies and fenugreek seeds and fry for 1 minute.

5 Lower the heat to medium and add the chicken pieces, together with their sauce, 2 or 3 pieces at a time. When all the chicken has been added to the wok, stir to mix well.

6 Simmer gently for 12–15 minutes or until the chicken is thoroughly cooked through.

7 Add the tomatoes, fresh cilantro and green chilies to the wok and serve immediately.

Balinese Spiced Duck

There is a delightful hotel on the beach at Sanur which cooks this delicious duck dish perfectly.

INGREDIENTS

Serves 4

8 duck portions, fat trimmed
   and reserved
¼ cup dried coconut
¾ cup coconut milk
salt and freshly ground black pepper
Deep-fried Onions and salad leaves or
   fresh herb sprigs, to garnish

For the spice paste

1 small onion or 4–6 shallots, sliced
2 garlic cloves, sliced
½ inch fresh ginger root, peeled
   and sliced
½ inch fresh *laos*, peeled and sliced
1 inch fresh turmeric or
   ½ teaspoon ground turmeric
1–2 red chilies, seeded and sliced
4 macadamia nuts or 8 almonds
1 teaspoon coriander seeds, dry-fried

1 Place the duck fat trimmings in a heated frying pan, and render the fat over a low heat. Reserve the fat.

2 Dry-fry the dried coconut in a preheated pan until crisp and brown in color.

3 To make the spice paste, blend the onion or shallots, garlic, ginger, *laos*, fresh or ground turmeric, chilies, nuts and coriander seeds to a paste in a food processor or with a mortar and pestle.

4 Spread the spice paste over the duck portions and let marinate in a cool place for 3–4 hours. Preheat the oven to 325°F. Shake off and reserve the spice paste, then transfer the duck breasts to an oiled roasting pan. Cover with a double layer of foil and cook the duck breasts in the preheated oven for 2 hours.

5 Turn the oven temperature up to 375°F. Heat the reserved duck fat in a pan, add the spice paste and fry for 1–2 minutes. Stir in the coconut milk and simmer for 2 minutes. Discard the duck juices then cover the duck with the spice mixture and sprinkle with the toasted coconut. Cook in the oven for 20–30 minutes.

6 Arrange the duck on a warm serving platter and sprinkle with the Deep-fried Onions. Season to taste and serve with the salad leaves or fresh herb sprigs of your choice.

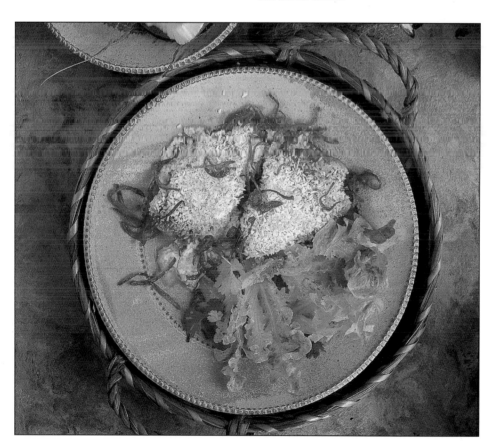

Duck with Chinese Mushrooms and Ginger

In Indonesia ducks are often seen, comically herded in single file, along the water channels between the rice paddies. The Chinese are particularly fond of duck and the delicious ingredients in this recipe gives it an oriental flavor.

INGREDIENTS

Serves 4

1 duck (about 5½ pounds)
1 teaspoon sugar
¼ cup light soy sauce
2 garlic cloves, crushed
8 dried Chinese mushrooms, soaked in
   1½ cups warm water for 30 minutes
1 onion, sliced
2 inches fresh ginger, sliced and cut in
   matchsticks
7 ounces baby corn
3–4 scallions, white parts left whole,
   green tops sliced
1–2 tablespoons cornstarch, mixed to a
   paste with 4 tablespoons water
salt and ground black pepper
boiled rice, to serve

2 Strain the mushrooms, reserving the soaking liquid. Trim and discard the stalks.

3 Fry the onion and ginger in the duck fat, in a frying pan, until they give off a good aroma. Push to one side. Lift the duck pieces out of the soy sauce and fry them until browned. Add the mushrooms and reserved liquid.

4 Add 2½ cups of the duck stock or water to the browned duck pieces. Season, cover and cook over a gentle heat for about 1 hour, or until the duck is tender.

5 Add the corn and the white part of the scallions and cook for another 10 minutes. Remove from the heat and add the cornstarch paste. Return to the heat and bring to a boil, stirring. Cook for about 1 minute until glossy. Sprinkle with the sliced scallion tops and serve with boiled rice.

1 Cut the duck along the breast, open it up and cut along each side of the backbone. Use the backbone, wings and giblets to make a stock, to use later in the recipe. Any trimmings of fat can be rendered in a frying pan, to use later in the recipe. Cut each leg and each breast in half. Place in a bowl, rub with the sugar and then pour over the soy sauce and garlic.

COOK'S TIP

Replace the corn with chopped celery and slices of drained, canned water chestnuts.

Sweet-and-sour Duck with Mango

Mango adds natural sweetness to this colorful stir-fry. Crispy deep-fried noodles make the perfect accompaniment.

INGREDIENTS

Serves 4

3 duck breasts (8–12 ounces total)
3 tablespoons dark soy sauce
1 tablespoon Chinese rice wine or dry sherry
1 teaspoon sesame oil
1 teaspoon five-spice powder
1 tablespoon brown sugar
2 teaspoons cornstarch
3 tablespoons Chinese rice vinegar
1 tablespoon ketchup
1 mango, not too ripe
3 baby eggplants
1 red onion
1 carrot
¼ cup peanut oil
1 garlic clove, sliced
1-inch piece fresh ginger, cut into shreds
3 ounces sugar-snap peas

1 Thinly slice the duck breasts and place in a bowl. Combine 1 tablespoon of the soy sauce with the rice wine or sherry, sesame oil and five-spice powder. Pour it over the duck, cover and let marinate for 1–2 hours. In a separate bowl, blend the sugar, cornstarch, rice vinegar, ketchup and remaining soy sauce. Set aside.

2 Peel the mango, slice the flesh from the pit, then cut into thick strips. Slice the eggplants, onion and carrot into similar-size pieces.

3 Heat a wok until hot, add 2 tablespoons of the oil and swirl it around. Drain the duck, reserving the marinade. Stir-fry the duck slices over high heat until the fat is crisp and golden. Remove and keep warm. Add 1 tablespoon of the oil to the wok and stir-fry the eggplants for 3 minutes until golden.

4 Add the remaining oil and fry the onion, garlic, ginger and carrot for 2–3 minutes, then add the sugar-snap peas and stir-fry for another 2 minutes.

5 Add the mango and return the duck with the sauce and reserved marinade to the wok. Cook, stirring, until the sauce thickens slightly. Serve immediately.

COOK'S TIP

If baby eggplants are not available, use the smallest eggplants you can find. Sprinkle with salt after slicing and set aside in a colander for the bitter juices to drain off. Rinse thoroughly before cooking.

Stir-fried Turkey with Broccoli and Mushrooms

This is a very easy, tasty supper dish that works well with chicken too.

INGREDIENTS

Serves 4

4 ounces broccoli florets
4 scallions
1 teaspoon cornstarch
3 tablespoons oyster sauce
1 tablespoon dark soy sauce
$1/2$ cup chicken stock
2 teaspoons lemon juice
3 tablespoons peanut oil
1 pound turkey cutlets, cut into
  $1/4$ x 2-inch strips
1 small onion, chopped
2 garlic cloves, crushed
2 teaspoons grated fresh ginger
1 cup fresh shiitake mushrooms, sliced
1 cup baby corn, halved lengthwise
1 tablespoon sesame oil
salt and ground black pepper
egg noodles, to serve

1 Divide the broccoli florets into smaller sprigs and cut the stalks into thin diagonal slices.

2 Finely chop the white parts of the scallions and slice the green parts into thin shreds.

3 In a bowl, combine the cornstarch, oyster sauce, soy sauce, stock and lemon juice. Set aside.

4 Heat 2 tablespoons of the peanut oil in a preheated wok. Add the turkey and stir-fry for 2 minutes, until golden and crisp at the edges. Remove from the wok and keep warm.

5 Add the remaining peanut oil to the wok and stir-fry the chopped onion, garlic and ginger over medium heat for about 1 minute. Increase the heat to high, add the broccoli, mushrooms and corn and stir-fry for 2 minutes.

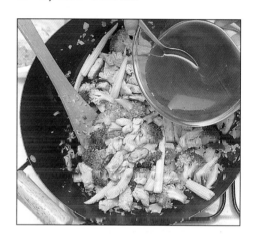

6 Return the turkey to the wok, then add the sauce with the chopped scallion and seasoning. Cook, stirring, for about 1 minute, until the sauce has thickened. Stir in the sesame oil. Serve immediately on a bed of egg noodles with the finely shredded scallion scattered on top.

> ——— COOK'S TIP ———
> Cook fresh egg noodles in salted boiling water, stirring occasionally to prevent them from sticking. They are ready within a few minutes. Follow the package instructions for cooking dried egg noodles.

VEGETABLE DISHES

Vegetables particularly benefit from fast cooking in a wok, as this helps to preserve their texture and color, as well as their nutritional content. This exciting collection of recipes includes some standard and familiar accompaniments to main-course dishes, such as potatoes, broccoli and onions, and also suggests some unusual vegetable dishes with more exotic ingredients and sauces. All of them are cooked in intriguing ways that lend themselves to Asian meals as well as to more traditional Western roasts, grilled meat and fish dishes.

Stir-fried Bok Choy with Mushrooms

You can use fresh button mushrooms in this recipe if you prefer them, or if fresh or canned straw mushrooms are not available.

Ingredients

Serves 4

1½ cups fresh straw mushrooms or 12-ounce can straw mushrooms, drained
¼ cup vegetable oil
1 head bok choy, cut into strips
1 teaspoon salt
1 teaspoon light brown sugar
1 tablespoon cornstarch paste
½ cup milk

1 Cut the mushrooms in half lengthwise. Heat half the oil, stir-fry the bok choy for 2 minutes, then add half the salt and half the sugar. Stir for 1 minute.

2 Transfer the bok choy to a warm serving dish. Add the mushrooms to the wok and stir-fry for 1 minute. Add the remaining salt and sugar, cook for 1 minute, then thicken with the cornstarch paste and milk. Serve with the bok choy.

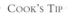

—————— Cook's Tip ——————

The Chinese approach to cooking illustrates the same overall desire for harmony and balance that characterizes their ancient philosophy. Recipes for stir-fried vegetables are not simply an arbitrary combination of whatever is at hand—they should balance and complement each other in both color and texture. The delicious slipperiness of straw mushrooms complements the crunchier texture of the bok choy, so it is best to use them if at all possible. Canned straw mushrooms are available at Asian food stores. Do not overcook, or the harmony and balance will be lost.

Stir-fried Bean Sprouts

This is an easy way to cook up some tasty bean sprouts in a wok. It is not necessary to trim them. Simply rinse in a bowl of cold water and discard any husks that float to the surface.

INGREDIENTS

Serves 4
2–3 scallions
3 tablespoons vegetable oil
2 cups bean sprouts
1 teaspoon salt
½ teaspoon light brown sugar
few drops of sesame oil (optional)

1 Cut the scallions into short sections about the same length as the bean sprouts.

2 Heat the oil in a wok and stir-fry the bean sprouts and scallions for about 1 minute. Add the salt and sugar and continue stirring for 1 minute. Sprinkle with the sesame oil, if using, and serve. Do not overcook, or the bean sprouts will become soggy.

COOK'S TIP

Fresh and canned bean sprouts are readily available, but they can easily be grown at home for a constant and completely fresh supply. Scatter mung beans on several layers of damp paper towels on a small plate. Keep moist in a fairly warm place, and the beans will sprout in a few days.

Braised Chinese Vegetables

The original recipe calls for no fewer than 18 different ingredients to represent the 18 Buddhas (*lo han*). Later, this was reduced to eight, but nowadays anything between four and six items is regarded as quite sufficient to put in a wok.

INGREDIENTS

Serves 4

¼ cup dried Chinese mushrooms
1 cup straw mushrooms
½ cup sliced bamboo shoots, drained
2 ounces snow peas
3-inch block fresh tofu
6 ounces bok choy leaves
3–4 tablespoons vegetable oil
1 teaspoon salt
½ teaspoon light brown sugar
1 tablespoon light soy sauce
few drops of sesame oil

1 Soak the Chinese mushrooms in warm water for 30 minutes, then rinse and discard the hard stalks, if any. Cut the straw mushrooms in half lengthwise if they are large; keep them whole if they are small. Rinse and drain the bamboo-shoot slices. Trim the snow peas. Cut the tofu into about 12 small pieces. Cut the bok choy into small pieces about the same size as the snow peas.

2 Harden the tofu pieces by placing them in a wok of boiling water for about 2 minutes. Remove and drain.

3 Discard the water and heat the oil in the wok, a saucepan or a flameproof casserole. Lightly brown the tofu pieces on both sides. Remove with a slotted spoon and keep warm.

4 Stir-fry all the vegetables in the wok for 1½ minutes, then add the tofu, salt, sugar and soy sauce. Continue stirring for 1 minute, then cover and braise for 2–3 minutes. Sprinkle with sesame oil and serve.

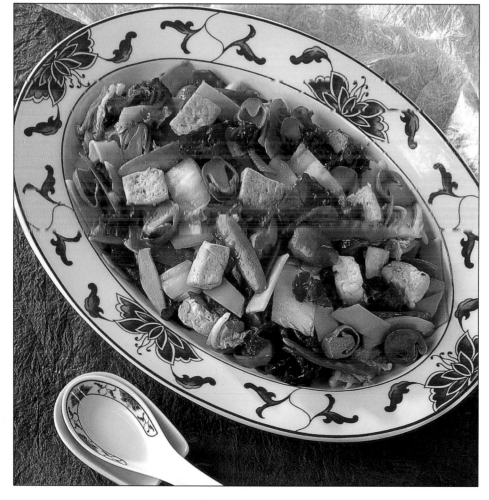

Eggplant in Spicy Sauce

Eggplant is given a royal treatment in this recipe, where it is stir-fried with seasonings more commonly associated with fish cooking.

INGREDIENTS

Serves 4

1 pound eggplants
3–4 dried red chilies, soaked in water
    for 10 minutes
vegetable oil, for deep-frying
1 garlic clove, finely chopped
1 teaspoon finely chopped fresh ginger
1 teaspoon finely chopped scallion,
    white part only
4 ounces lean pork, thinly shredded
    (optional)
1 tablespoon light soy sauce
1 tablespoon light brown sugar
1 tablespoon chili bean sauce
1 tablespoon Chinese rice wine or
    dry sherry
1 tablespoon rice vinegar
2 teaspoons cornstarch paste,
1 teaspoon finely chopped scallions,
    green part only, to garnish
few drops of sesame oil

1 Cut the eggplants into short strips the size of french fries—the skin can either be peeled off or left on, whichever you prefer. Cut the soaked red chilies into two or three small pieces and discard the seeds.

2 Heat the oil in a preheated wok and deep-fry the eggplant strips for 3–4 minutes or until limp. Remove and drain.

3 Pour off the excess oil, leaving about 1 tablespoon in the wok. Add the garlic, ginger, white scallions and chilies, stir a few times, then add the pork, if using. Stir-fry the meat for about 1 minute or until it becomes pale, almost white, in color. Add all the seasonings, then increase the heat and bring the mixture to a boil.

4 Add the eggplants to the wok, blend well and braise for 30–40 seconds, then thicken the sauce with the cornstarch paste, stirring until smooth. Garnish with the green scallions and sprinkle with sesame oil.

--- COOK'S TIP ---

Soaking dried chilies in water will reduce their spicy flavor. If you prefer a milder chili taste, soak for longer than the recommended 10 minutes.

Szechuan Spicy Tofu

The meat used in this popular
wok recipe can be omitted to
create a purely vegetarian dish, if
you prefer.

INGREDIENTS

Serves 4
3-inch block fresh tofu
1 leek
3 tablespoons vegetable oil
4 ounces ground beef
1 tablespoon black bean sauce
1 tablespoon light soy sauce
1 teaspoon chili bean sauce
1 tablespoon Chinese rice wine or
  dry sherry
3–4 tablespoons stock or water
2 teaspoons cornstarch paste
ground Szechuan peppercorns, to taste
few drops of sesame oil

1 Cut the tofu into ½-inch square
cubes. Fill a wok with boiling
water, add the tofu cubes and bring
back to a boil. Cook for 2–3 minutes
to harden. Remove and drain. Cut the
leek into short sections.

2 Empty the wok. Preheat and
add the oil. When hot, stir-fry the
ground beef until the color changes,
then add the leek and black bean sauce.
Add the tofu with the soy sauce, chili
bean sauce and wine or sherry. Stir
gently for 1 minute.

3 Add the stock or water, bring to a
boil and braise for 2–3 minutes.

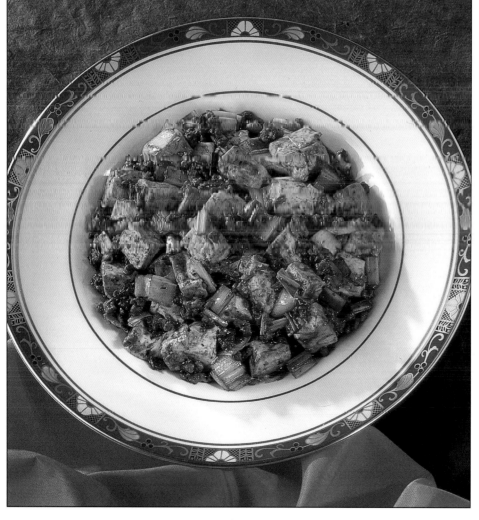

4 Stir in the cornstarch paste and
cook, stirring, until thickened.
Season with ground Szechuan pepper,
sprinkle with the sesame oil and serve
immediately.

Karahi Shredded Cabbage with Cumin

This cabbage is only lightly spiced and makes a good accompaniment to most other Indian dishes.

INGREDIENTS

Serves 4

1 tablespoon corn oil
4 tablespoons butter
½ teaspoon crushed coriander seeds
½ teaspoon white cumin seeds
6 dried red chilies
1 small Savoy cabbage, shredded
12 snow peas
3 fresh red chilies, seeded and sliced
12 ears baby corn
salt
1 ounce slivered almonds, toasted, and
    1 tablespoon chopped fresh cilantro
    (optional), to garnish

1 Heat the oil and butter in a preheated wok and, when the butter has melted, add the crushed coriander seeds, cumin seeds and dried red chilies.

2 Add the shredded cabbage and snow peas to the wok and stir-fry for about 5 minutes.

3 Add the fresh red chilies, baby corn and salt and stir-fry for a further 3 minutes.

4 Garnish the cabbage with toasted almonds and fresh cilantro, if using, and serve hot.

---— COOK'S TIP —---

Unlike many parts of the Indian sub-continent, Pakistan, where this dish originates, is generally a meat-eating nation. Vegetable dishes are, therefore, usually cooked as side dishes, rather than as a main dish, much in the way they are in the West. Consequently, this delicious, slightly spicy treatment of cabbage would go as well with a traditional Western roast as it would with an Indian curry or stir-fry.

Spicy Indian Potatoes

Potatoes often are an integral part of an Indian meal. Rice is not always served, or it may be served in addition to potatoes, which are frequently treated as just another vegetable rather than as a staple.

INGREDIENTS

Serves 4

3 tablespoons corn oil
½ teaspoon white cumin seeds
3 curry leaves
1 teaspoon crushed dried red chilies
½ teaspoon mixed onion, mustard and fenugreek seeds
½ teaspoon fennel seeds
3 garlic cloves, thinly sliced
½ teaspoon shredded fresh ginger
2 medium onions, sliced
6 new potatoes, cut into ¼-inch slices
1 tablespoon chopped fresh cilantro
1 fresh red chili, seeded and sliced
1 fresh green chili, seeded and sliced

1 Heat the oil in a preheated wok. When hot, lower the heat and add the cumin seeds, curry leaves, dried red chilies, onion, mustard and fenugreek seeds, fennel seeds, garlic and ginger. Stir-fry for about 1 minute, then add the onions and fry for 5 minutes or until the onions are golden brown.

2 Add the potatoes, cilantro and fresh red and green chilies to the wok and mix well. Cover tightly with a lid or foil, making sure the foil does not touch the food. Cook over very low heat for about 7 minutes or until the potatoes are tender.

3 Remove the lid or foil and serve in the traditional manner—straight from the pot.

Okra with Green Mango and Lentils

If you like okra, you will love this tangy and spicy dish.

INGREDIENTS

Serves 4

½ cup yellow lentils
3 tablespoons corn oil
½ teaspoon onion seeds
2 medium onions, sliced
½ teaspoon ground fenugreek
1 teaspoon grated fresh ginger
1 teaspoon crushed garlic
1½ teaspoon chili powder
¼ teaspoon ground turmeric
1 teaspoon ground coriander
1 unripe mango, peeled and pitted
1 pound okra, chopped
2 fresh red chilies, seeded and sliced
2 tablespoons chopped fresh cilantro
1 tomato, sliced

1 Wash the lentils thoroughly and put in a saucepan with just enough water to cover. Bring to a boil and cook until soft but not mushy. Drain and set aside.

2 Heat the oil in a preheated wok. Add the onion seeds and fry until they begin to pop. Add the onions and fry until they are golden brown. Lower the heat and add the ground fenugreek, ginger, garlic, chili powder, ground turmeric and ground coriander.

3 Slice the mango, then add with the okra. Stir well and add the red chilies and fresh cilantro. Stir-fry for about 3 minutes or until the okra is well cooked. Stir in the cooked lentils and sliced tomato, then cook for another 3 minutes. Serve immediately.

Crispy Cabbage

This makes a wonderful accompaniment to meat or vegetable dishes—just a couple spoonfuls add a crunchy texture to a meal. It goes especially well with shrimp dishes.

Ingredients

Serves 4

4 juniper berries
1 large Savoy cabbage
¼ cup vegetable oil
1 clove garlic, crushed
1 teaspoon superfine sugar
1 teaspoon salt

1 Finely crush the juniper berries in a mortar with a pestle.

2 Finely shred the cabbage.

3 Heat a wok, then add the oil. When the oil is hot, stir-fry the garlic for 1 minute. Add the cabbage and stir-fry for 3–4 minutes, until crispy. Remove from the wok and pat dry with paper towels.

4 Reheat the wok and return the cabbage to it. Add the sugar, salt and crushed juniper berries and toss the cabbage until well coated and thoroughly mixed with the flavorings. Serve either hot or cold.

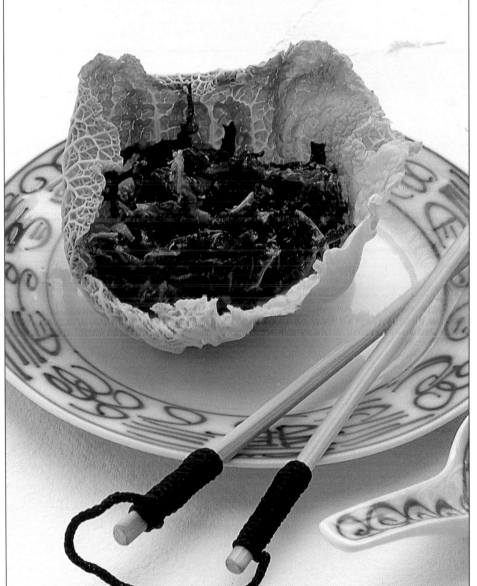

Stir-fried Greens

Quail's eggs look very attractive in *Chah Kang Kung*, but you can substitute some baby corn, halved at an angle.

INGREDIENTS

Serves 4

2 bunches spinach or chard or 1 head
   Chinese cabbage
3 garlic cloves, crushed
2 inches fresh ginger root, peeled and
   cut in matchsticks
3–4 tablespoons peanut oil
14 ounces boneless, skinless chicken
   breast, or pork loin, or a mixture of
   both, very finely sliced
12 quail's eggs, hard-boiled and shelled
1 fresh red chili, seeded and shredded
2–3 tablespoons oyster sauce
1 tablespoon brown sugar
2 teaspoons cornstarch, mixed with
   ¼ cup cold water
salt

COOK'S TIP

As with all stir-fries, don't start cooking until you have prepared all the ingredients and arranged them to hand. Cut everything into small, even-size pieces so the food can be cooked very quickly and all the colors and flavors preserved.

1 Wash the chosen leaves well and shake them dry. Strip the tender leaves from the stems and tear them into pieces. Discard the lower, tougher part of the stems and slice the remainder evenly.

2 Fry the garlic and ginger in the hot oil, without browning, for a minute. Add the chicken and/or pork and keep stirring it in the wok until the meat changes color. When the meat looks cooked, add the sliced stems first and cook them quickly; then add the torn leaves, quail's eggs and chili. Spoon in the oyster sauce and a little boiling water, if necessary. Cover and cook for 1–2 minutes only.

3 Remove the lid, stir and add sugar and salt to taste. Stir in the cornstarch and water mixture and toss thoroughly. Cook until the mixture is well coated in a glossy sauce.

4 Serve immediately, while still very hot and the colors are bright and glowingly jewel-like.

Water Spinach with Brown Bean Sauce

Water spinach, often known as Siamese watercress, is a green vegetable with arrowhead-shaped leaves. If you can't find it, use spinach, watercress, *bok choy* or even broccoli, and adjust the cooking time accordingly. There are excellent variations to this recipe using black bean sauce, instead of brown bean sauce.

INGREDIENTS

Serves 4–6
1 bunch water spinach, about
  2¼ pounds in weight
3 tablespoons vegetable oil
1 tablespoon chopped garlic
1 tablespoon brown bean sauce
2 tablespoons fish sauce
1 tablespoon sugar
freshly ground black pepper

1 Trim and discard the bottom coarse, woody end of the water spinach. Cut the remaining part into 2-inch lengths, keeping the leaves separate from the stems.

2 Heat the oil in a wok or large frying pan. When it starts to smoke, add the chopped garlic and toss for 10 seconds.

3 Add the stem part of the water spinach, let it sizzle and cook for 1 minute, then add the leafy parts.

4 Stir in the brown bean sauce, fish sauce, sugar and pepper. Toss and turn over the spinach until it begins to wilt, about 3–4 minutes. Transfer to a serving dish and serve immediately.

Mixed Vegetables in Coconut Milk

A most delicious way of cooking vegetables. If you don't like highly spiced food, use fewer red chili peppers.

INGREDIENTS

Serves 4–6
1 pound mixed vegetables, such as
  eggplant, baby canned corn, carrots,
  snake beans and patty pan squash
8 red chilies, seeded
2 lemongrass stalks, chopped
4 kaffir lime leaves, torn
2 tablespoons vegetable oil
1 cup unsweetened coconut milk
2 tablespoons fish sauce
a pinch of salt
15–20 Thai basil leaves, to garnish

1 Cut the vegetables into similar size shapes using a sharp knife.

2 Put the red chilies, lemongrass and kaffir lime leaves in a mortar and grind together with a pestle.

3 Heat the oil in a wok or large deep frying pan. Add the chili mixture and fry for 2–3 minutes.

4 Stir in the coconut milk and bring to a boil. Add the vegetables and cook for about 5 minutes, or until they are tender. Season with the fish sauce and salt, and garnish with basil leaves.

Szechuan Eggplants

INGREDIENTS

Serves 4

2 small eggplants
1 teaspoon salt
3 dried red chilies
peanut oil, for deep-frying
3–4 garlic cloves, finely chopped
½-inch piece fresh ginger, finely
    chopped
4 scallions, chopped and white and
    green parts separated
1 tablespoon Chinese rice wine or
    dry sherry
1 tablespoon light soy sauce
1 teaspoon sugar
¼ teaspoon ground roasted
    Szechuan peppercorns
1 tablespoon rice vinegar
1 teaspoon sesame oil

1 Trim the eggplants and cut into strips about 1½ inches wide and 3 inches long. Place the eggplants in a colander and sprinkle with the salt. Let sit for 30 minutes, then rinse them thoroughly under cold running water. Pat dry with paper towels.

2 Meanwhile, soak the chilies in warm water for 15 minutes. Drain, then cut each chili into three or four pieces, discarding the seeds.

3 Half-fill a wok with oil and heat to 350°F. Deep-fry the eggplants, in batches if necessary, until golden brown. Drain on paper towels. Pour off most of the oil from the wok. Reheat the oil and add the garlic, ginger and white part of the scallions.

4 Stir-fry for 30 seconds. Add the eggplants and toss, then add the wine or sherry, soy sauce, sugar, ground peppercorns and vinegar. Stir-fry for 1–2 minutes. Sprinkle on the sesame oil and scallion greens.

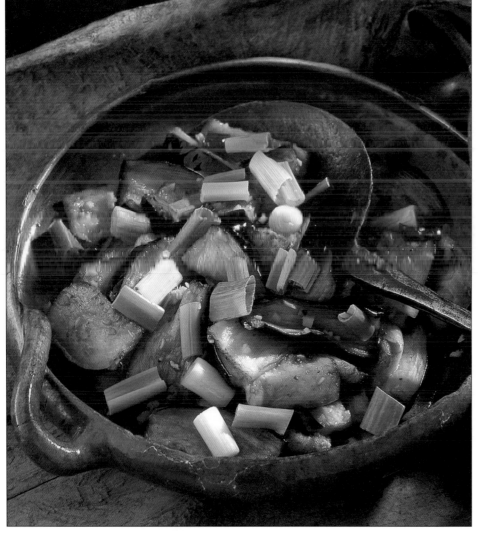

Root Vegetables with Spiced Salt

All kinds of root vegetables can be finely sliced and deep fried to make "chips." Serve as an accompaniment to an Asian-style meal or simply by themselves as much tastier nibbles than store-bought snacks with predinner drinks.

INGREDIENTS

Serves 4–6
1 carrot
2 parsnips
2 raw beets
1 sweet potato
peanut oil, for deep-frying
¼ teaspoon chili powder
1 teaspoon sea salt flakes

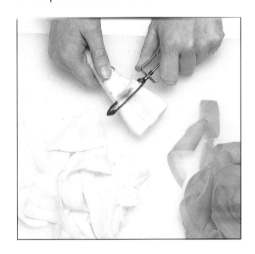

1 Peel the carrot, parsnips, beets and sweet potato. Slice the carrot and parsnips into long, thin ribbons. Cut the beets and sweet potato into thin rounds. Pat dry with paper towels.

2 Half-fill a wok with oil and heat to 350°F. Add the vegetable slices in batches and deep-fry for 2–3 minutes, until golden and crisp. Remove and drain on paper towels.

3 Place the chili powder and sea salt flakes in a mortar and grind them together with a pestle to form a coarse powder.

4 Pile the vegetable "chips" on a serving plate and sprinkle with the spiced salt.

--- COOK'S TIP ---

To save time, you can slice the vegetables using a mandoline, blender or food processor with a thin slicing disc attached.

Spiced Cauliflower Braise

A delicious vegetable stew, known as *Sambal Kol Kembang,* which combines coconut milk with spices and is perfect as a vegetarian main course or as part of a buffet.

INGREDIENTS

Serves 4
1 cauliflower
2 medium or 1 large tomato(es)
1 onion, chopped
2 garlic cloves, crushed
1 fresh green chili, seeded
1/2 tablespoon ground turmeric
1/2 teaspoon shrimp paste
2 tablespoons sunflower oil
14-fluid ounce can coconut milk
1 cup water
1 teaspoon sugar
1 teaspoon tamarind pulp, soaked in
   3 tablespoons warm water
salt

1 Trim the stalk from the cauliflower and divide into tiny florets. Skin the tomato(es) if liked. Chop the flesh into 1/2–1-inch pieces.

2 Grind the chopped onion, garlic, green chili, ground turmeric and shrimp paste together to a paste in a food processor or with a mortar and pestle. Heat the sunflower oil in a wok or large frying pan and fry the spice paste to bring out the aromatic flavors, without allowing it to brown.

3 Add the cauliflower florets and toss well to coat in the spices. Stir in the coconut milk, water, sugar and salt to taste. Simmer for 5 minutes. Strain the tamarind and reserve the juice.

4 Add the tamarind juice and chopped tomatoes to the pan then cook for 2–3 minutes only. Taste for check the seasoning and serve.

Spicy Scrambled Eggs

This is a lovely way to liven up scrambled eggs. When making *Orak Arik,* prepare all the ingredients ahead so that the vegetables retain all their crunch and color.

INGREDIENTS

Serves 4
2 tablespoons sunflower oil
1 onion, finely sliced
8 ounces Chinese cabbage, finely sliced
   or cut in diamonds
7-ounce can corn kernels
1 small fresh red chili, seeded and finely
   sliced (optional)
2 tablespoons water
2 eggs, beaten
salt and freshly ground black pepper
Deep-fried Onions, to garnish

1 Heat a wok, add the oil and fry the onion, until soft but not browned.

2 Add the Chinese cabbage and toss well together. Add the corn, chili and water. Cover with a lid and cook for 2 minutes.

3 Remove the lid and stir in the beaten eggs and the seasoning. Stir constantly until the eggs are creamy and just set. Serve on warmed plates, sprinkled with crisp Deep-fried Onions.

Spiced Coconut Mushrooms

Here is a simple and delicious way to cook mushrooms. They can be served with almost any Asian meal, as well as with traditional Western grilled or roasted meats and poultry.

Ingredients

Serves 4

2 tablespoons peanut oil
2 garlic cloves, finely chopped
2 fresh red chilies, seeded and sliced into rings
3 shallots, finely chopped
2 cups Crimini mushrooms, thickly sliced
²/₃ cup coconut milk
2 tablespoons chopped fresh cilantro
salt and ground black pepper

1 Heat a wok until hot, add the oil and swirl it around the wok. Add the garlic and chilies, then stir-fry for a few seconds.

— Cook's Tip —

Use snipped fresh chives instead of chopped fresh cilantro, if desired.

2 Add the shallots and stir-fry for 2–3 minutes, until softened. Add the mushrooms and stir-fry for 3 minutes.

3 Pour in the coconut milk and bring to a boil. Boil rapidly over high heat until the liquid has reduced by about half and coats the mushrooms. Season to taste with salt and pepper.

4 Sprinkle the chopped cilantro on top and toss the mushrooms gently to mix. Serve immediately.

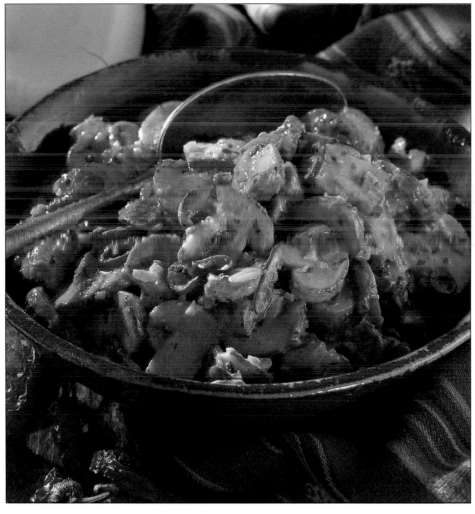

Mixed Vegetable Pickle

If you can obtain fresh turmeric, it makes such a difference to the color and appearance of *Acar Campur*. You can use almost any vegetable, bearing in mind that you need a balance of textures, flavors and colors.

INGREDIENTS

Makes 2–3 11-ounce jars
1 fresh red chili, seeded and sliced
1 onion, quartered
2 garlic cloves, crushed
½ teaspoon shrimp paste
4 macadamia nuts or 8 almonds
1 inch fresh turmeric, peeled and
   sliced, or 1 teaspoon ground turmeric
¼ cup sunflower oil
2 cups white vinegar
1 cup water
3–6 tablespoons granulated sugar
3 carrots
8 ounces green beans
1 small cauliflower
1 cucumber
8 ounces white cabbage
¾ cup dry-roasted peanuts,
   roughly crushed
salt

1 Place the chili, onion, garlic, shrimp paste, nuts and turmeric in a food processor and blend to a paste, or pound in a mortar with a pestle.

2 Heat the oil and stir-fry the paste to release the aroma. Add the vinegar, water, sugar and salt. Bring to a boil. Simmer for 10 minutes.

3 Cut the carrots into flower shapes. Cut the green beans into short, neat lengths. Separate the cauliflower into neat, bite-size florets. Peel and seed the cucumber and cut the flesh in neat, bite-size pieces. Cut the cabbage in neat, bite-size pieces.

4 Blanch each vegetable separately, in a large pan of boiling water, for 1 minute. Transfer to a colander and rinse with cold water, to halt the cooking. Drain well.

--- COOK'S TIP ---

This pickle is even better if you make it a few days ahead.

5 Add the vegetables to the sauce. Slowly bring to a boil and allow to cook for 5–10 minutes. Do not overcook – the vegetables should still be crunchy.

6 Add the peanuts and cool. Spoon into clean jars with lids.

Black Bean and Vegetable Stir-fry

The secret of a quick stir-fry is proper preparation of all the ingredients first. It is important that the ingredients are added to the wok in the right order, so that the larger or thicker pieces have a longer cooking time than the smaller pieces—even if this is a difference of only a fraction of an inch and a few seconds!

INGREDIENTS

Serves 4

1 1/2 cups scallions
8 ounces button mushrooms
1 red bell pepper
1 green bell pepper
2 large carrots
1/2 cup sesame oil
2 garlic cloves, crushed
1/4 cup black bean sauce
6 tablespoons warm water
1 cup bean sprouts
salt and ground black pepper

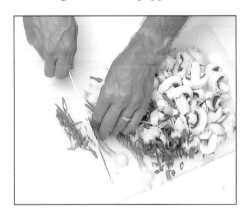

1 Thinly slice the scallions and button mushrooms.

2 Cut both the bell peppers in half, remove the seeds and slice the flesh into thin strips.

3 Cut the carrots in half. Cut each half into thin strips lengthwise. Stack the slices and cut through them to make very fine strips.

4 Heat the oil in a large preheated wok until very hot. Add the scallions and garlic and stir-fry for 30 seconds.

5 Add the mushrooms, bell peppers and carrots. Stir-fry for 5–6 minutes over high heat, until the vegetables are just beginning to soften.

6 Mix the black bean sauce with the water. Add to the wok and cook for 3–4 minutes. Stir in the bean sprouts and cook for 1 more minute, until all the vegetables are coated in the sauce. Season to taste, then serve immediately.

COOK'S TIP

Black bean sauce is made from salted black beans—which have a very distinctive flavor—that have been crushed and mixed with a variety of spices, such as ginger and chili. It is quite a thick paste and readily available in jars, bottles and cans at large supermarkets and Asian food stores. Store in the refrigerator after opening.

Stir-fried Spinach with Garlic and Sesame Seeds

The sesame seeds add a crunchy texture that contrasts well with the wilted spinach in this easy vegetable dish.

INGREDIENTS

Serves 2
½ bunch fresh spinach, washed
1½ tablespoons sesame seeds
2 tablespoons peanut oil
¼ teaspoon sea salt
2–3 garlic cloves, sliced

COOK'S TIP

Take care when adding the spinach to the hot oil, as it will spit furiously.

1 Shake the spinach to get rid of any excess water, then remove the stalks and discard any yellow or damaged leaves. Lay several spinach leaves one on top of another, roll up tightly and cut horizontally into wide strips. Repeat with the remaining leaves.

2 Heat a wok to medium heat, add the sesame seeds and dry-fry, stirring constantly, for 1–2 minutes, until golden brown. Transfer to a small bowl and set aside.

3 Add the oil to the wok and swirl it around. When hot, add the salt, spinach and garlic and stir-fry for 2 minutes, until the spinach just wilts and the leaves are coated in oil.

4 Sprinkle the dry-fried sesame seeds on top and toss well. Serve immediately.

Bok Choy with Oyster Sauce

Here, bok choy is prepared in a very simple way—stir-fried and served with oyster sauce. This Cantonese combination makes a simple, quickly prepared and tasty accompaniment to Asian or Western seafood dishes. Vegetarians may prefer to substitute light soy or hoisin sauce for the oyster sauce used in this recipe.

INGREDIENTS

Serves 3–4
1 head bok choy
2 tablespoons peanut oil
1–2 tablespoons oyster sauce

1 Trim the bok choy and tear into manageable pieces.

2 Heat a wok until hot, add the oil and swirl it around.

3 Add the bok choy and stir-fry for 2–3 minutes, until it has wilted a little.

COOK'S TIP

You can replace the bok choy with Chinese flowering cabbage, which is also known by its Cantonese name *choi sam*. It has bright green leaves and tiny yellow flowers, which are eaten along with the leaves and stalks. It is available at Asian supermarkets.

4 Add the oyster sauce and continue to stir-fry for a few more seconds, until the bok choy is cooked but still slightly crisp. Serve immediately.

Tofu Stir-fry

The tofu has a pleasant creamy texture, which contrasts delightfully with the crunchy stir-fried vegetables. Make sure you buy firm tofu that is easy to cut neatly.

INGREDIENTS

Serves 2–4

4 ounces white cabbage
2 fresh green chilies
8-ounce package fresh firm tofu
3 tablespoons vegetable oil
2 garlic cloves, crushed
3 scallions, chopped
6 ounces green beans, trimmed
1 cup baby corn, halved
½ cup bean sprouts
3 tablespoons smooth peanut butter
1½ tablespoons dark soy sauce
1¼ cups coconut milk

2 Using a sharp knife, cut the tofu into thin strips.

3 Heat a wok, then add 2 tablespoons of the oil. When the oil is hot, add the tofu, stir-fry for 3 minutes and remove. Set aside. Wipe out the wok with paper towels.

4 Add the remaining oil to the wok. When it is hot, add the garlic, scallions and chilies and stir-fry for 1 minute. Then add the green beans, corn and bean sprouts and stir-fry for 2 more minutes.

5 Add the peanut butter and soy sauce to the wok. Stir well to coat the vegetables. Add the tofu to the vegetables in the wok.

6 Pour the coconut milk over the vegetables, simmer for 3 minutes and serve immediately.

1 Shred the cabbage. Carefully remove the seeds from the chilies and chop finely.

COOK'S TIP

There are literally hundreds of varieties of chili. Generally speaking, dark green chilies are hotter than paler green ones, which are, in turn, hotter and less sweet than red chilies—but this is not a hard-and-fast rule and it is possible to be fooled by an unfamiliar variety. The "heat factor" of chilies is measured in Scoville units, with bell peppers at 0, at the bottom of the scale, and Mexican habanero chilies at 300,000, the hottest, at the top. Most Asian recipes call for medium to hot chilies. Some Indonesian and Thai dishes can be very fiery, but Chinese recipes tend to use fairly mild fresh green or red chilies.

Cooked Vegetable Gado-gado

Instead of putting everything on a large platter, you can serve individual servings of this salad. It is a perfect recipe for lunchtime or informal gatherings.

INGREDIENTS

Serves 6

8 ounces waxy potatoes, cooked
1 pound mixed cabbage, spinach and
   bean sprouts, in equal proportions,
   rinsed and shredded
½ cucumber, cut in wedges, salted and
   set aside for 15 minutes
2–3 eggs, hard-cooked and shelled
4 ounces fresh tofu
oil, for frying
6–8 large shrimp crackers
lemon juice
Deep-fried Onions, to garnish
Peanut Sauce, see Vegetable Salad with
   Hot Peanut Sauce

1 Cube the potatoes and set aside. Bring a large pan of salted water to a boil. Plunge one type of raw vegetable at a time into the pan for just a few seconds to blanch. Lift out the vegetables with a large slotted spoon and hold under very cold running water, or plunge them into iced water and set aside for 2 minutes. Drain thoroughly. Blanch all the vegetables, except the cucumber, in this way.

2 Rinse the cucumber pieces and drain them well. Cut the eggs in quarters. Cut the tofu into cubes.

3 Fry the tofu in hot oil in a wok until crisp on both sides. Lift out and drain on paper towels.

4 Add more oil to the pan and then deep-fry the shrimp crackers one or two at a time. Reserve them on a tray lined with paper towels.

5 Arrange all the cooked vegetables attractively on a platter, with the cucumber, hard-cooked eggs and tofu. Sprinkle with the lemon juice and garnish with the Deep-fried Onions.

6 Serve with peanut sauce and hand round the fried shrimp crackers separately.

Spicy Zucchini Fritters with Thai Salsa

The Thai salsa goes just as well with plain stir-fried salmon strips or stir-fried beef as it does with these zucchini fritters.

INGREDIENTS

Serves 2–4
2 teaspoons cumin seeds
2 teaspoons coriander seeds
1 pound zucchini
1 cup gram flour
½ teaspoon baking soda
salt and ground black pepper
½ cup peanut oil
fresh mint sprigs, to garnish

For the Thai salsa
½ cucumber, diced
3 scallions, chopped
6 radishes, cubed
2 tablespoons chopped fresh mint
1 inch piece fresh ginger, peeled
  and grated
3 tablespoons lime juice
2 tablespoons superfine sugar
3 garlic cloves, crushed

1 Heat a wok, then dry-fry the cumin and coriander seeds. Cool them, then grind well, using a mortar and pestle.

COOK'S TIP

You can substitute daikon, also known as mooli or white radish, for the round radishes in the salsa.

---

2 Cut the zucchini into 3-inch sticks. Place in a bowl.

3 Process the flour, baking soda, spices and salt and pepper in a food processor or blender. Add 1 cup warm water with 1 tablespoon of the peanut oil and process again.

4 Coat the zucchini in the batter, then let stand for 10 minutes.

5 To make the salsa, combine the cucumber, scallions, radishes, mint, ginger and lime juice in a bowl. Stir in the sugar and garlic.

6 Heat the wok, then add the remaining oil. When the oil is hot, stir-fry the zucchini in batches. Drain well on paper towels, then serve hot with the Thai salsa, garnished with fresh mint sprigs.

Spiced Vegetables with Coconut

This spicy and substantial stir-fry could be served as an appetizer, or as a vegetarian main course for two. Eat it with spoons and forks, and provide hunks of whole-grain bread for mopping up the delicious coconut milk.

INGREDIENTS

Serves 2–4
1 fresh red chili
1 fennel bulb
2 large carrots
6 celery stalks
2 tablespoons peanut oil
1-inch piece fresh ginger, peeled
    and grated
1 garlic clove, crushed
3 scallions, sliced
14-ounce can thin coconut milk
1 tablespoon chopped fresh cilantro
salt and ground black pepper
fresh cilantro sprigs, to garnish

----- COOK'S TIP -----

When buying fennel, look for well-rounded bulbs; flatter ones are immature and will not have developed their full aniseed-like flavor. The bulbs should be white with overlapping ridged layers. Avoid any that look damaged or bruised. The fennel should be dry, but not desiccated.

1 Halve, seed and finely chop the chili.

2 Thinly slice the carrots and the celery stalks on the diagonal.

3 Trim the fennel bulb and slice roughly, using a sharp knife.

4 Heat a wok, then add the peanut oil. When the oil is hot, add the chili, fennel, carrots, celery, ginger, garlic and scallions and stir-fry for 2 minutes.

5 Stir in the coconut milk with a large spoon and bring to a boil.

6 Stir in the chopped cilantro and salt and pepper, and serve garnished with cilantro sprigs.

Bok Choy and Mushroom Stir-fry

Try to buy all the varieties of mushroom for this dish—wild oyster and shiitake mushrooms have particularly distinctive, delicate flavors that work well when stir-fried.

INGREDIENTS

Serves 4

4 dried black Chinese mushrooms
⅔ cup hot water
1 head bok choy
½ cup oyster mushrooms, preferably wild
½ cup shiitake mushrooms
1 tablespoon vegetable oil
1 garlic clove, crushed
2 tablespoons oyster sauce

1 Soak the black Chinese mushrooms in the hot water for 30 minutes to soften. Drain, and discard the tough stalks.

COOK'S TIP

Bok choy, also called pok choi and Chinese white cabbage, is an attractive member of the cabbage family, with long, smooth, white stems and dark green leaves. It has a pleasant flavor that does not in any way resemble that of cabbage.

2 Tear the bok choy into bite-size pieces with your fingers.

3 Halve any large oyster and shiitake mushrooms, using a sharp knife.

4 Heat a wok, then add the oil. When the oil is hot, stir-fry the garlic until softened but not colored.

5 Add the bok choy to the wok and stir-fry for 1 minute. Mix in all the mushrooms and stir-fry for 1 minute.

6 Add the oyster sauce, toss well and serve immediately.

Red-cooked Tofu with Chinese Mushrooms

"Red-cooked" is a term applied to Chinese dishes cooked with a dark soy sauce. This tasty dish can be served as either a side dish or a main course.

Ingredients

Serves 4

8-ounce package fresh firm tofu
3 tablespoons dark soy sauce
2 tablespoons Chinese rice wine or
    dry sherry
2 teaspoons dark brown sugar
1 garlic clove, crushed
1 tablespoon grated fresh ginger
½ teaspoon five-spice powder
pinch of ground roasted Szechuan
    peppercorns
6 dried black Chinese mushrooms
1 teaspoon cornstarch
2 tablespoons peanut oil
5–6 scallions, sliced into 1-inch lengths,
    white and green parts separated
small fresh basil leaves, to garnish
rice noodles, to serve

2 Meanwhile, soak the dried black mushrooms in warm water for 30 minutes, until soft. Drain, reserving 6 tablespoons of the soaking liquid. Squeeze out any excess liquid from the mushrooms, remove the tough stalks and slice the caps. In a small bowl, blend the cornstarch with the reserved marinade and mushroom soaking liquid.

4 Add the mushrooms and white parts of the scallions to the wok and stir-fry for 2 minutes. Pour in the reserved marinade and stir for 1 minute, until thickened.

5 Return the tofu to the wok with the green parts of the scallions. Simmer gently for 1–2 minutes. Scatter the basil leaves on top and serve immediately with rice noodles.

1 Drain the tofu, pat dry with paper towels and cut into 1-inch cubes. Place in a shallow dish. In a small bowl, combine the soy sauce, rice wine or sherry, sugar, garlic, ginger, five-spice powder and Szechuan peppercorns. Pour the marinade over the tofu, toss well and let marinate for about 30 minutes. Drain, reserving the marinade.

3 Heat a wok until hot, add the oil and swirl it around. Add the tofu and stir-fry for 2–3 minutes, until evenly golden. Remove from the wok and set aside.

Pancakes with Stir-fried Vegetables

To serve, each person spreads a little hoisin sauce over a pancake, adds a helping of the filling from the wok and rolls up the pancake.

INGREDIENTS

Serves 4

3 eggs
2 tablespoons water
¼ cup peanut oil
¼ cup dried black Chinese mushrooms
¼ cup dried wood ear mushrooms
2 teaspoons cornstarch
2 tablespoons light soy sauce
2 tablespoons Chinese rice wine or dry sherry
2 teaspoons sesame oil
2 garlic cloves, finely chopped
½-inch piece fresh ginger, cut into thin shreds
½ cup canned sliced bamboo shoots, drained and rinsed
½ cup bean sprouts
4 scallions, finely shredded
salt and ground black pepper
fresh cilantro, to garnish
Chinese pancakes and hoisin sauce, to serve

1 Whisk the eggs, water and seasoning in a small bowl. Heat 1 tablespoon of the peanut oil in a wok and swirl it around. Pour in the eggs, then tilt the wok so that they spread into an even layer. Continue to cook over high heat for about 2 minutes, until set. Turn onto a board and, when cool, roll up the omelet and cut into thin strips. Wipe the wok clean.

COOK'S TIP

Chinese pancakes are available at Asian supermarkets. Reheat them in a bamboo steamer for 2–3 minutes just before serving.

2 Meanwhile, put the black Chinese mushrooms and wood ear mushrooms in separate bowls. Pour in enough warm water to cover, then let soak for 30 minutes, until soft. Drain the mushrooms, reserving their soaking liquid. Squeeze the excess liquid from each of them.

3 Remove the tough stalks and thinly slice the black mushrooms. Finely shred the wood ears. Set aside. Strain the reserved soaking liquid through cheesecloth into a bowl; reserve ½ cup of the liquid. In a bowl, blend the cornstarch with the reserved liquid, soy sauce, rice wine or sherry and sesame oil.

4 Heat the wok over medium heat, add the remaining peanut oil and swirl it around. Add the wood ears and black mushrooms and stir-fry for about 2 minutes. Add the garlic, ginger, bamboo shoots and bean sprouts and stir-fry for 1–2 minutes.

5 Pour in the cornstarch mixture and cook, stirring, for 1 minute, until thickened. Add the scallions and omelet strips and toss gently. Adjust the seasoning, adding more soy sauce, if needed. Serve immediately with the Chinese pancakes, garnished with cilantro, and accompanied by the hoisin sauce.

Stir-fried Vegetables with Cilantro Omelet

A wok is the ideal utensil for cooking an omelet, as the heat is evenly distributed over the wide surface. This is a great supper dish for vegetarians. The glaze is intended to give the vegetables an appealing shine and does not constitute a sauce.

INGREDIENTS

Serves 3–4

For the omelet

2 eggs
2 tablespoons water
3 tablespoons chopped fresh cilantro
salt and ground black pepper
1 tablespoon peanut oil

For the glazed vegetables

1 tablespoon cornstarch
2 tablespoons Chinese rice wine or dry sherry
1 tablespoon sweet chili sauce
½ cup vegetable stock
2 tablespoons peanut oil
1 teaspoon grated fresh ginger
6–8 scallions, sliced
4 ounces snow peas
1 yellow bell pepper, seeded and sliced
½ cup fresh shiitake or button mushrooms
½ cup canned water chestnuts, drained and rinsed
½ cup bean sprouts
½ small head bok choy, roughly shredded

COOK'S TIP

Vary the combination of vegetables used according to availability and taste, but make sure that you slice or chop them to approximately the same size and thickness.

1 To make the omelet, whisk the eggs, water, cilantro and seasoning in a small bowl. Heat the oil in a wok. Pour in the eggs, then tilt the wok so that the mixture spreads in an even layer. Cook over high heat until the edges are slightly crisp.

2 Flip the omelet over with a spatula and cook the other side for about 30 seconds until lightly browned. Turn the omelet onto a board and let cool. When cool, roll up loosely and cut into thin slices. Wipe the wok clean.

3 In a bowl, blend the cornstarch, wine or sherry, chili sauce and stock to make the glaze. Set aside.

4 Heat the wok until hot, add the oil and swirl it around. Add the ginger and scallions and stir-fry for a few seconds to flavor the oil. Add the snow peas, sliced bell pepper, mushrooms and water chestnuts and stir-fry for 3 minutes.

5 Add the bean sprouts and bok choy and stir-fry for 2 minutes.

6 Pour in the glaze mixture and cook, stirring, for about 1 minute, until the glaze thickens and coats the vegetables. Turn the vegetables onto a warmed serving plate and top with the omelet shreds. Serve immediately.

Broccoli in Oyster Sauce

The broccoli florets retain their vivid shade of green and crunchy texture, as well as much of their vitamin and mineral content, when given this wok treatment. Vegetarians may prefer to substitute light soy sauce for the oyster sauce.

INGREDIENTS

Serves 4

1 large bunch broccoli
3–4 tablespoons vegetable oil
½ teaspoon salt
½ teaspoon light brown sugar
2–3 tablespoons vegetable stock
   or water
2 tablespoons oyster sauce or light
   soy sauce

1 Cut the broccoli heads into small florets. Remove the rough skin from the stalks and cut them into even-size chunks.

2 Heat the oil in a preheated wok and add the salt, then stir-fry the broccoli for about 2 minutes. Add the sugar and stock or water, and continue stirring for 1 minute. Add the oyster or soy sauce, blend well and serve.

—————— COOK'S TIP ——————

Always choose healthy-looking broccoli with firm stems that are neither woody nor wrinkled. Look for tightly packed, nicely colored flower heads with no signs of yellowing. Broccoli is best eaten on the day it is purchased or, better still, picked. It deteriorates rapidly in storage and loses many of the vitamins for which it is especially valued, as well as its crispness.

Deep-fried Onions

Known as *bawang goreng*, these are a traditional accompaniment and garnish to many Indonesian dishes. Asian stores sell them ready-made, but it is simple to make them at home, using fresh onions. The small red onions that can be bought at Asian food stores are excellent when deep-fried, as they contain less water than most European varieties.

INGREDIENTS

Makes 1 pound
1 pound onions
oil for deep-frying

1 Peel the onions and slice as evenly and finely as possible.

2 Spread out thinly on paper towels in an airy place and let dry for 30 minutes to 2 hours.

3 Heat the oil in a wok to 375°F. Deep-fry the onions in batches, turning them all the time, until they are crisp and golden. Drain well on paper towels and cool. Deep-fried onions may be stored in an airtight container.

--- COOK'S TIP ---

Garlic can be prepared and cooked in the same way, or some can be fried with the last batch of onions. Deep-fried garlic gives an added dimension of flavor as a garnish for many dishes.

An even faster way to prepare homemade deep-fried onions is to use a 3-ounce package of quick-dried onions, which you can fry in about 1 cup sunflower oil. This gives you 4 ounces of fried onion flakes.

Bamboo Shoots and Chinese Mushrooms

Another name for this dish is "twin winter vegetables," because both bamboo shoots and mushrooms are at their best in winter. For that reason, try using canned winter bamboo shoots and extra "fat" mushrooms.

INGREDIENTS

Serves 4
½ cup dried Chinese mushrooms
10-ounce can winter bamboo shoots
3 tablespoons vegetable oil
1 scallion, cut into short sections
2 tablespoons light soy sauce or
   oyster sauce
1 tablespoon Chinese rice wine or
   dry sherry
½ teaspoon light brown sugar
2 teaspoons cornstarch paste
few drops of sesame oil

1 Soak the mushrooms in warm water for 30 minutes. Drain, squeeze dry and discard any hard stalks, reserving the water. Cut the mushrooms in half or in quarters if they are large—keep them whole if small.

2 Rinse and drain the bamboo shoots, then cut them into small, wedge-shaped pieces.

3 Heat the oil in a preheated wok and stir-fry the mushrooms and bamboo shoots for about 1 minute. Add the scallion, soy or oyster sauce, wine or sherry and the sugar with 2–3 tablespoons of the reserved mushroom liquid. Bring to a boil and braise for 1–2 minutes. Stir in the cornstarch paste to thicken, sprinkle with the sesame oil and serve.

Stir-fried Tomatoes, Cucumber and Eggs

The cucumber can be replaced by a green bell pepper or zucchini if you prefer.

INGREDIENTS

Serves 4
4 large firm tomatoes, skinned
½ cucumber, unpeeled
4 eggs
1 teaspoon salt
1 scallion, finely chopped
¼ cup vegetable oil
2 teaspoons Chinese rice wine or dry
   sherry (optional)

1 Cut the tomatoes and cucumber in half lengthwise, then cut horizontally into small wedges. In a bowl, beat the eggs with a pinch of salt and a few pieces of the chopped scallion.

2 Heat about half the oil in a preheated wok, then pour in the eggs and scramble lightly over medium heat until set but not too dry. Remove the scrambled egg from the wok and keep warm.

3 Add the remaining oil to the wok and heat over high heat. Add the vegetables and stir-fry for 1 minute. Add the remaining salt, then the scrambled eggs and wine or sherry, if using. Serve immediately.

SALADS

Stir-frying is a good way of creating some interesting and unusual salads, as flavors can be blended without any loss of the all-important crispness and texture. Vegetables, seafood, chicken and noodles are just some of the ingredients that can be combined to make delicious summer meals or refreshing side dishes to serve at any time of year. Try the tantalizing Vegetable Salad with Hot Peanut Sauce, the mouthwatering combination of fish and spices in a traditional Thai Seafood Salad or the terrific, crunchy Curry Fried Pork and Rice Vermicelli Salad.

Tofu and Cucumber Salad

Tahu goreng ketjap is a nutritious and refreshing salad with a hot sweet-and-sour dressing. It is ideal for buffets.

INGREDIENTS

Serves 4–6
1 small cucumber
oil, for frying
1 square fresh or 4 ounces
 long-life tofu
4 ounces bean sprouts, trimmed
 and rinsed
salt

For the dressing
1 small onion, grated
2 garlic cloves, crushed
½ teaspoon chili powder
2–3 tablespoons dark soy sauce
1–2 tablespoons rice wine vinegar
2 teaspoons dark brown sugar
salt
celery leaves, to garnish

1 Trim the ends from the cucumber and then cut it in neat cubes. Sprinkle with salt and set aside, while preparing the remaining ingredients.

2 Heat a little oil in a pan and fry the tofu on both sides until golden brown. Drain on paper towels and cut in cubes.

COOK'S TIP

Bean sprouts come from the mung bean and are easily grown at home on damp cotton or in a plastic bean sprouter. They must be eaten when absolutely fresh, so when buying from a shop check that they are crisp and are not beginning to go brown or soft. Eat within a day or two.

3 Prepare the dressing by blending together the onion, garlic and chili powder. Stir in the soy sauce, vinegar, sugar and salt to taste. You can do this in a screw-top glass jar.

4 Just before serving, rinse the cucumber under cold running water. Drain and dry thoroughly. Toss the cucumber, tofu and bean sprouts together in a serving bowl and pour over the dressing. Garnish with the celery leaves and serve the salad at once.

Vegetable Salad with Hot Peanut Sauce

A wok is ideal for dry-frying as well as stir-frying, and here it is used to great effect in making this wonderful peanut sauce.

INGREDIENTS

Serves 4–6
2 potatoes, peeled
6 ounces green beans, trimmed

For the peanut sauce
¾ cup peanuts
1 tablespoon vegetable oil
2 shallots or 1 small onion,
    finely chopped
1 garlic clove, crushed
1–2 small fresh chilies, seeded and
    finely chopped
½-inch square shrimp paste, or
    1 tablespoon fish sauce (optional)
2 tablespoons tamarind sauce
⅓ cup canned coconut milk
1 tablespoon honey

For the salad
2 heads bok choy, shredded
1 head iceberg or Bibb lettuce,
    separated into leaves
1 cup bean sprouts, washed
½ cucumber, cut into fingers
5 ounces daikon, shredded
3 scallions, trimmed
8-ounce package fresh tofu, cut into
    large dice
3 hard-cooked eggs, quartered

1 Bring the potatoes to a boil in salted water and simmer for 20 minutes. Add the beans and cook for 3–4 minutes. Drain the potatoes and beans under cold running water.

2 For the peanut sauce, dry-fry the peanuts in a wok, or place under a medium broiler, tossing them constantly to prevent burning. Turn the peanuts onto a clean dish towel and rub vigorously to remove the papery skins. Place the peanuts in a food processor or blender and process for 2 minutes.

3 Heat the oil in a wok and soften the shallots or onion, garlic and chilies without letting them color. Add the shrimp paste or fish sauce, if using, together with the tamarind sauce, coconut milk and honey. Simmer briefly, add to the peanuts and process in a food processor to form a thick sauce.

4 Arrange the salad ingredients, potatoes and beans on a large platter and serve with a bowl of the peanut sauce.

Thai Seafood Salad

This seafood salad with chili, lemongrass and fish sauce is light and refreshing.

INGREDIENTS

Serves 4
8 ounces ready-prepared squid
8 ounces uncooked shrimp
8 scallops, shelled
8 ounces firm white fish
2–3 tablespoons olive oil
small mixed lettuce leaves and
    cilantro sprigs, to serve

For the dressing
2 small fresh red chilies, seeded and
    finely chopped
2-inch piece lemongrass, finely
    chopped
2 kaffir lime leaves, shredded
2 tablespoons fish sauce
2 shallots, thinly sliced
2 tablespoons lime juice
2 tablespoons rice vinegar
2 teaspoons superfine sugar

1 Prepare the seafood. Slit open the squid bodies. Score the flesh with a sharp knife, then cut into square pieces. Halve the tentacles, if necessary. Shell and devein the shrimp. Remove the dark beardlike fringe and tough muscle from the scallops. Cube the white fish.

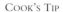
— COOK'S TIP —

It is important to ensure that the shrimp are cooked properly, as undercooked shrimp can carry infection.

2 Heat a wok until hot. Add the oil and swirl it around, then add the shrimp and stir-fry for 2–3 minutes, until pink. Transfer to a large bowl. Stir-fry the squid and scallops for 1–2 minutes, until opaque. Remove and add to the shrimp. Stir-fry the white fish for 2–3 minutes. Remove and add to the cooked seafood. Reserve any juices.

3 Put all the dressing ingredients in a small bowl with the reserved juices from the wok; mix well.

4 Pour the dressing over the seafood and toss gently. Arrange the salad leaves and cilantro sprigs on four individual plates, then spoon the seafood on top. Serve immediately.

Cabbage Salad

A simple and delicious way of using cabbage. Other vegetables such as broccoli, cauliflower, beansprouts and Chinese cabbage can also be prepared this way.

INGREDIENTS

Serves 4–6

2 tablespoons fish sauce
grated rind of 1 lime
2 tablespoons lime juice
½ cup unsweetened coconut milk
2 tablespoons vegetable oil
2 large red chilies, seeded and finely cut into strips
6 garlic cloves, finely sliced
6 shallots, finely sliced
1 small cabbage, shredded
2 tablespoons coarsely chopped roasted peanuts, to serve

1 Make the dressing by combining the fish sauce, lime rind and juice and coconut milk. Set aside.

2 Heat the oil in a wok or frying pan. Stir-fry the chilies, garlic and shallots, until the shallots are brown and crisp. Remove and set aside.

3 Blanch the cabbage in boiling salted water for about 2–3 minutes, drain and put into a bowl.

4 Stir the dressing into the cabbage, toss and mix well. Transfer the salad to a serving dish. Sprinkle with the fried shallot mixture and the chopped roasted peanuts.

Hot-and-sour Chicken Salad

INGREDIENTS

Serves 4–6

2 boneless chicken breasts, skinned
1 small fresh red chili, seeded and
  finely chopped
½-inch piece fresh ginger, peeled
  and finely chopped
1 garlic clove, chopped
1 tablespoon crunchy peanut butter
2 tablespoons chopped fresh cilantro
1 teaspoon sugar
½ teaspoon salt
1 tablespoon rice vinegar or white
  wine vinegar
¼ cup vegetable oil
2 teaspoons fish sauce
  (optional)
½ cup bean sprouts
1 head bok choy, roughly shredded
2 medium carrots, cut into
  thin sticks
1 red onion, cut into fine rings
2 large gherkins, sliced

1 Slice the chicken thinly, place in a shallow bowl and set aside. Grind the chili, ginger and garlic in a mortar with a pestle. Add the peanut butter, cilantro, sugar and salt.

2 Add the vinegar, 2 tablespoons of the oil and the fish sauce, if using. Combine well. Cover the chicken with the spice mixture and let marinate for at least 2–3 hours.

3 Heat the remaining oil in a preheated wok. Add the chicken and cook for 10–12 minutes, turning the meat occasionally. Meanwhile, arrange the bean sprouts, bok choy, carrots, onion rings and gherkins decoratively on a serving platter. Serve the chicken arranged on the salad.

Alfalfa Crab Salad with Crispy Fried Noodles

INGREDIENTS

Serves 4–6

vegetable oil, for deep-frying
2 ounces Chinese rice noodles
5 ounces white crabmeat
½ cup alfalfa sprouts
1 small head iceberg lettuce
4 sprigs fresh cilantro, roughly chopped
1 tomato, skinned, seeded and diced
4 sprigs fresh mint, roughly chopped

For the sesame lime dressing

3 tablespoons vegetable oil
1 tablespoon sesame oil
½ fresh red chili, seeded and chopped
1 piece preserved ginger in syrup, cut
  into matchsticks
2 teaspoons preserved ginger syrup
2 teaspoons soy sauce
juice of ½ lime

1 To make the dressing, combine the vegetable and sesame oils in a bowl. Add the chili, ginger, ginger syrup and soy sauce with the lime juice.

2 Heat the oil in a preheated wok to 375°F. Deep-fry the noodles, one handful at a time, until crisp. Lift out and drain on paper towels.

3 Flake the crabmeat into a bowl and mix well with the alfalfa sprouts. Put the lettuce, cilantro, tomato and mint in a serving bowl, pour on the dressing and toss lightly. Place a nest of noodles on top and finally add the crab and alfalfa sprouts.

Egg Noodle Salad with Sesame Chicken

INGREDIENTS

Serves 4–6

14 ounces fresh, thin egg noodles
1 carrot, cut into long fine strips
2 ounces snow peas, ends removed, cut
   into fine strips and blanched
4 ounces bean sprouts, blanched
2 tablespoons olive oil
8 ounces skinless, boneless chicken
   breasts, finely sliced
2 tablespoons sesame seeds, toasted
2 scallions, finely sliced diagonally
   and cilantro leaves, to garnish

For the dressing

3 tablespoons sherry vinegar
5 tablespoons soy sauce
4 tablespoons sesame oil
6 tablespoons light olive oil
1 garlic clove, finely chopped
1 teaspoon grated fresh ginger
salt and freshly ground black pepper

1 To make the dressing, combine all the ingredients in a small bowl with a pinch of salt, and mix together well using a whisk or a fork.

2 Cook the noodles in a large saucepan of boiling water. Stir them occasionally to separate. They will only take a few minutes to cook: be careful not to overcook them. Drain, rinse under cold running water, and drain well. Turn into a bowl.

3 Add the vegetables to the noodles. Pour in about half the dressing, then toss the mixture well. Adjust the seasoning according to taste.

4 Heat the oil in a large frying pan. Add the chicken, and stir-fry for 3 minutes, or until cooked and golden. Remove from the heat. Add the sesame seeds, and drizzle in some of the remaining dressing.

5 Arrange the noodles on individual serving plates, making a nest on each plate. Spoon the chicken on top. Sprinkle with the sliced scallions and the cilantro leaves. Serve any remaining dressing separately.

Potato and Cellophane Noodle Salad

INGREDIENTS

Serves 4

2 potatoes, peeled and cut
   into eighths
6 ounces cellophane noodles, soaked in
   hot water until soft
4 tablespoons vegetable oil
1 onion, finely sliced
1 teaspoon ground turmeric
4 tablespoons gram flour
1 teaspoon grated lemon rind
4–5 tablespoons lemon juice
3 tablespoons fish sauce
4 scallions, finely sliced
salt and freshly ground black pepper

1 Place the potatoes in a saucepan.
Add water to cover, bring to a boil,
and cook for about 15 minutes until
tender but firm. Drain the potatoes,
then set them aside to cool.

2 Meanwhile, cook the drained
noodles in a saucepan of boiling
water for 3 minutes. Drain, and rinse
under cold running water. Drain well.

3 Heat the oil in a frying pan. Add
the onion and turmeric, and fry for
about 5 minutes until golden brown.
Drain the onion, reserving the oil.

4 Heat a small frying pan. Add the
gram flour, and stir constantly for
about 4 minutes until it turns light
golden brown in color.

5 Mix the potatoes, noodles and
fried onion in a large bowl. Add
the reserved oil and the toasted gram
flour with the lemon rind and juice,
fish sauce and scallions. Mix together
well, and adjust the seasoning to taste,
if necessary. Serve at once.

Curry Fried Pork and Rice Vermicelli Salad

Pork crackles add a delicious crunch to this popular salad.

INGREDIENTS

Serves 4

8 ounces lean pork
2 garlic cloves, finely chopped
2 slices fresh ginger, finely chopped
2–3 tablespoons rice wine
3 tablespoons vegetable oil
2 lemon grass stalks,
   finely chopped
2 teaspoons curry powder
6 ounces bean sprouts
8 ounces rice vermicelli, soaked in
   warm water until soft
½ lettuce, finely shredded
2 tablespoons mint leaves
lemon juice and fish sauce, to taste
salt and freshly ground black pepper
2 scallions, chopped, 2 tablespoons
   roasted peanuts, chopped, and pork
   crackles (optional), to garnish

1 Cut the pork into thin strips. Place in a shallow dish with half the garlic and ginger. Season with salt and pepper, pour over 2 tablespoons rice wine, and marinate for at least 1 hour.

2 Heat the oil in a frying pan. Add the remaining garlic and ginger, and fry for a few seconds until fragrant. Stir in the pork, with the marinade, and add the lemon grass and curry powder. Fry until the pork is golden and cooked through, adding more rice wine if the mixture seems too dry.

3 Place the bean sprouts in a strainer. Blanch them by lowering the strainer into a pan of boiling water for 1 minute, then drain and refresh under cold running water. Drain again. Using the same water, cook the drained rice vermicelli for 3–5 minutes until tender, drain, and rinse under cold running water. Drain well. Turn into a bowl.

4 Add the bean sprouts, shredded lettuce and mint leaves to the rice vermicelli. Season with the lemon juice and fish sauce. Toss lightly.

5 Divide the noodle mixture among individual serving plates, making a nest on each plate. Arrange the pork mixture on top. Garnish with the chopped scallions, roasted peanuts and pork crackles, if using.

Larp of Chiang Mai

Chiang Mai is a city in the north-east of Thailand. The city is culturally very close to Laos and famous for its chicken salad, which was originally called *Laap* or *Larp*. Duck, beef or pork can be used instead.

INGREDIENTS

Serves 4–6
1 pound ground chicken
1 lemongrass stalk, finely chopped
3 kaffir lime leaves, finely chopped
4 red chilies, seeded and chopped
4 tablespoons lime juice
2 tablespoons fish sauce
1 tablespoon roasted ground rice
2 scallions, chopped
2 tablespoons cilantro leaves
mixed salad leaves, cucumber and
    tomato slices, to serve
a few sprigs of mint, to garnish

1 Heat a large non-stick frying pan. Add the ground chicken and cook in a little water.

COOK'S TIP

Use sticky, or glutinous, rice to make roasted ground rice. Firstly put the rice in a frying pan and dry-roast it until golden brown. Remove and grind it to a powder in a mortar and pestle or in a food processor. Keep in a glass jar in a cool and dry place and use as required.

2 Stir constantly for about 7–10 minutes until cooked.

3 Transfer the cooked chicken to a large bowl and add the rest of the ingredients. Mix thoroughly.

4 Serve on a bed of mixed salad leaves, cucumber and tomato slices and garnish with sprigs of mint.

NOODLES

*There are many different sorts of
noodles, and the ways in which they
can be served are virtually endless, as
they combine so well with almost all
other kinds of ingredients. For the busy
cook, they have the added advantage of
being both quick and easy to prepare.
The recipes here have been inspired by
the cuisines of many countries,
sometimes marrying Western and Asian
flavors in colorful and inventive dishes.
Discover the versatility of noodles with
dishes such as Buckwheat Noodles with
Goat Cheese, Crispy Noodles with
Mixed Vegetables or Bamie Goreng.*

Vegetable and Egg Noodle Ribbons

Serve this elegant, colorful dish with a tossed green salad as a light lunch or as an appetizer for six to eight people.

INGREDIENTS

Serves 4

1 large carrot, peeled
2 zucchini
4 tablespoons butter
1 tablespoon olive oil
6 fresh shiitake mushrooms, finely sliced
½ cup frozen peas, thawed
12 ounces broad egg noodle ribbons
2 teaspoons chopped mixed fresh herbs (such as marjoram, chives and basil)
salt and freshly ground black pepper
1 ounce Parmesan cheese, to serve (optional)

1 Using a vegetable peeler, carefully slice thin strips from the carrot and from the zucchini.

2 Heat the butter with the olive oil in a large frying pan. Stir in the carrots and shiitake mushrooms. Fry for 2 minutes. Add the zucchini and peas, and stir-fry until the zucchini are cooked, but still crisp. Season with salt and pepper.

3 Meanwhile, cook the noodles in a large saucepan of boiling water until just tender. Drain the noodles well, and turn them into a bowl. Add the vegetables, and toss to mix.

4 Sprinkle over the fresh herbs, and season to taste. If using the Parmesan cheese, grate or shave it over the top. Toss lightly, and serve.

Buckwheat Noodles with Goat Cheese

When you don't feel like doing a lot of cooking, try this good, fast supper dish. The earthy flavor of buckwheat goes well with the nutty, peppery taste of arugula leaves, offset by the deliciously creamy goat cheese.

INGREDIENTS

Serves 4

12 ounces buckwheat noodles
4 tablespoons butter
2 garlic cloves, finely chopped
4 shallots, sliced
½ cup hazelnuts, lightly roasted and coarsely chopped
large handful arugula leaves
6 ounces goat cheese
salt and freshly ground black pepper

1 Cook the noodles in a large saucepan of boiling water until just tender. Drain well.

2 Heat the butter in a large frying pan. Add the garlic and shallots, and cook for 2–3 minutes, stirring constantly, until the shallots are soft.

3 Add the hazelnuts, and fry for about 1 minute. Add the arugula leaves and, when they start to wilt, toss in the noodles, and heat through.

4 Season with salt and pepper. Crumble in the goat cheese, and serve immediately.

Shanghai Noodles with Lap Cheong

Lap cheong are firm, cured, waxy pork sausages, available in Chinese food markets. Sweet and savory, they can be steamed with rice, chicken or pork, added to an omelet or stir-fried with a variety of vegetables.

INGREDIENTS

Serves 4

2 tablespoons vegetable oil
4 ounces Canadian bacon, cut into bite-size pieces
2 lap cheong, rinsed in warm water, drained and finely sliced
2 garlic cloves, finely chopped
2 scallions, coarsely chopped
8 ounces chard or fresh spinach leaves, cut into 2-inch pieces
1 pound fresh Shanghai noodles
2 tablespoons oyster sauce
2 tablespoons soy sauce
freshly ground black pepper

1 Heat half the oil in a wok or large frying pan. Add the bacon and lap cheong with the garlic and scallions. Stir-fry for a few minutes until golden. Using a slotted spoon, remove the mixture from the wok or pan, and keep warm.

2 Add the remaining oil to the wok or pan. When hot, stir-fry the chard or spinach over a high heat for about 3 minutes until it starts to wilt.

3 Add the noodles, and return the lap cheong mixture to the wok or pan. Season with oyster sauce, soy sauce and pepper. Stir-fry until the noodles are heated through.

COOK'S TIP

There are many types of Chinese greens available. They include broccoli, rape and red and green chard.

Noodles with Tomatoes, Sardines and Mustard

Serve this simple dish hot or at room temperature.

INGREDIENTS

Serves 4

12 ounces broad egg noodles
4 tablespoons olive oil
2 tablespoons lemon juice
1 tablespoon whole-grain mustard
1 garlic clove, finely chopped
8 ounces ripe tomatoes, coarsely chopped
1 small red onion, finely chopped
1 green bell pepper, seeded and finely diced
4 tablespoons chopped parsley
8 ounces canned sardines, drained
salt and freshly ground black pepper
croûtons, made from 2 slices of bread, to serve (optional)

1 Cook the noodles in a large saucepan of boiling water for about 5–8 minutes until just tender.

2 Meanwhile, to make the dressing, whisk the oil, lemon juice, mustard and garlic in a small bowl with salt and pepper to taste.

3 Drain the noodles, turn them into a large bowl, and toss with the dressing. Add the tomatoes, onion, pepper, parsley and sardines, and toss lightly again. Season to taste, and serve with crisp croûtons, if using.

Special Chow Mein

Lap cheong is a special air-dried Chinese sausage. It is available from most Chinese markets. If you cannot buy it, substitute with either diced ham, chorizo sausage or salami.

INGREDIENTS

Serves 4–6
3 tablespoons vegetable oil
2 garlic cloves, sliced
1 teaspoon chopped fresh ginger
2 red chilies, chopped
2 lap cheong, about 3 ounces, rinsed
    and sliced (optional)
1 boneless chicken breast, thinly sliced
16 uncooked jumbo shrimp, peeled,
    tails left intact, and deveined
1 cup green beans
1 cup bean sprouts
2 ounces garlic chives
1 pound egg noodles, cooked in
    boiling water until tender
2 tablespoons soy sauce
1 tablespoon oyster sauce
1 tablespoon sesame oil
salt and freshly ground black pepper
2 scallions, shredded, to garnish
1 tablespoon cilantro leaves,
    to garnish

2 Heat the rest of the oil in the same wok. Add the bean sprouts and garlic chives. Stir-fry for 1–2 minutes.

4 Return the shrimp mixture to the wok. Reheat and mix well with the noodles. Stir in the sesame oil. Serve garnished with scallions and cilantro leaves.

1 Heat 1 tablespoon of the oil in a wok or large frying pan and fry the garlic, ginger and chilies. Add the lap cheong, chicken, shrimp and beans. Stir-fry for about 2 minutes over high heat or until the chicken and shrimp are cooked. Transfer the mixture to a bowl and set aside.

3 Add the noodles and toss and stir to mix. Season with soy sauce, oyster sauce, salt and pepper.

Chicken Chow Mein

Chow Mein is arguably the best known Chinese noodle dish in the West. To make it, noodles are stir-fried with meat, seafood or vegetables.

INGREDIENTS

Serves 4

12 ounces noodles
8 ounces skinless, boneless chicken breasts
3 tablespoons soy sauce
1 tablespoon rice wine or dry sherry
1 tablespoon dark sesame oil
4 tablespoons vegetable oil
2 garlic cloves, finely chopped
2 ounces snow peas, ends removed
4 ounces bean sprouts
2 ounces ham, finely shredded
4 scallions, finely chopped
salt and freshly ground black pepper

1 Cook the noodles in a saucepan of boiling water until tender. Drain, rinse under cold water, and drain well.

2 Slice the chicken into fine, 2-inch shreds. Place in a bowl. Add 2 teaspoons of the soy sauce, the rice wine or sherry and sesame oil.

3 Heat half the vegetable oil in a wok or large frying pan over a high heat. When the oil starts smoking, add the chicken mixture. Stir-fry for about 2 minutes, then transfer the chicken to a plate, and keep it hot.

4 Wipe the wok clean, and heat the remaining oil. Stir in the garlic, snow peas, bean sprouts and ham, stir-fry for another minute or so, and add the noodles.

5 Continue to stir-fry until the noodles are heated through. Add the remaining soy sauce to taste, and season with salt and pepper. Return the chicken and any juices to the noodle mixture, add the scallions, and give the mixture a final stir. Serve at once.

Vegetarian Fried Noodles

When making this dish for non-vegetarians, or for vegetarians who eat fish, add a piece of *blacan* (compressed shrimp paste). A small chunk about the size of a bouillon cube, mashed with the chili paste, will add a deliciously rich, aromatic flavor.

INGREDIENTS

Serves 4

2 eggs
1 teaspoon chili powder
1 teaspoon turmeric
4 tablespoons vegetable oil
1 large onion, finely sliced
2 red chilies, seeded and
  finely sliced
1 tablespoon soy sauce
2 large cooked potatoes, cut into
  small cubes
6 pieces fried bean curd (tofu), sliced
8 ounces bean sprouts
4 ounces green beans, blanched
12 ounces fresh thick egg noodles
salt and freshly ground black pepper
sliced scallions, to garnish

1 Beat the eggs lightly, then strain them into a bowl. Heat a lightly greased omelet pan. Pour in half of the egg to cover the bottom of the pan thinly. When the egg is just set, turn the omelet over, and fry the other side briefly. Slide onto a plate, blot with paper towels, roll up, and cut into narrow strips. Make a second omelet in the same way, and slice it. Set the omelet strips aside for the garnish.

— COOK'S TIP —

Fried bean curd can be found in the refrigerated section of most good Asian food markets. It will keep for several days after opening.

2 In a cup, mix together the chili powder and turmeric. Form a paste by stirring in a little water.

3 Heat the oil in a wok or large frying pan. Fry the onion until soft. Reduce the heat, and add the chili paste, sliced chilies and soy sauce. Fry for 2–3 minutes.

4 Add the potatoes, and fry for about 2 minutes, mixing well with the chilies. Add the bean curd, then the bean sprouts, green beans and noodles.

5 Gently stir-fry until the noodles are evenly coated and heated through. Take care not to break up the potatoes or the bean curd. Season with salt and pepper. Serve hot, garnished with the reserved omelet strips and scallion slices.

Fried Cellophane Noodles

INGREDIENTS

Serves 4

6 ounces cellophane noodles
3 tablespoons vegetable oil
3 garlic cloves, finely chopped
4 ounces cooked shrimp, peeled
2 lap cheong, rinsed, drained and
  finely diced
2 eggs
2 celery stalks, including leaves, diced
4 ounces bean sprouts
4 ounces spinach, cut into large pieces
2 scallions, chopped
1–2 tablespoons fish sauce
1 teaspoon sesame oil
1 tablespoon sesame seeds, toasted,
  to garnish

1 Soak the cellophane noodles in hot water for about 10 minutes or until soft. Drain, and cut the noodles into 4-inch lengths.

2 Heat the oil in a wok, add the garlic, and fry until golden brown. Add the shrimp and lap cheong. Stir-fry for 2–3 minutes. Stir in the noodles, and fry for 2 minutes more.

3 Make a well in the center of the shrimp mixture, break in the eggs, and slowly stir them until they are creamy and just set.

COOK'S TIP

This is a very versatile dish. Vary the vegetables if you wish, and substitute ham, chorizo or salami for the lap cheong.

---

4 Stir in the celery, bean sprouts, spinach and scallions. Season with fish sauce, and stir in the sesame oil. Continue to stir-fry until all the ingredients are cooked, mixing well.

5 Transfer to a serving dish. Sprinkle with sesame seeds to garnish.

Crispy Noodles with Mixed Vegetables

In this dish, rice vermicelli noodles are deep-fried until crisp, then tossed with a colorful selection of stir-fried vegetables.

INGREDIENTS

Serves 4

2 large carrots
2 zucchini
4 scallions
4 ounces yard-long beans or
  green beans
4 ounces dried rice vermicelli or
  cellophane noodles
peanut oil, for deep frying
1-inch piece fresh ginger, shredded
1 fresh red chili, sliced
¾ cup fresh shiitake or button
  mushrooms, thickly sliced
few bok choy leaves, roughly shredded
⅓ cup bean sprouts
2 tablespoons light soy sauce
2 tablespoons Chinese rice wine or
  dry sherry
1 teaspoon sugar
2 tablespoons roughly torn fresh
  cilantro leaves

COOK'S TIP

Vermicelli rice noodles, which are thin and brittle, look like a bundle of white hair. They cook almost instantly in hot liquid, provided they have been first soaked in warm water. Rice noodles can also be deep-fried. Cellophane noodles, which are made from ground mung beans, look a little like bundles of cotton candy. They are opaque white when dried, and expand and become translucent after soaking. Cellophane noodles are also known as bean thread, transparent or glass noodles. Dried noodles must be soaked for 5 minutes in hot water before cooking.

1 Cut the carrots and zucchini into fine sticks. Shred the scallions into similar-sized pieces. Trim the beans and cut them into short lengths.

2 Break the noodles into lengths of about 3 inches. Half-fill a wok with oil and heat it to 350°F. Deep-fry the raw noodles, a handful at a time, for 1–2 minutes, until puffed and crispy. Drain on paper towels. Pour off all but 2 tablespoons of the oil.

3 Reheat the oil in the wok. When hot, add the beans and stir-fry for 2–3 minutes.

4 Add the ginger, red chili, mushrooms, carrots and zucchini and stir-fry for 1–2 minutes. Add the bok choy, bean sprouts and scallions. Stir-fry for 1 minute, then add the soy sauce, rice wine or sherry and sugar. Cook, stirring, for about 30 seconds.

5 Add the noodles and cilantro and toss to mix, taking care not to crush the noodles too much. Serve immediately, piled on a plate.

Mee Krob

This delicious dish makes a filling meal. Be careful when frying rice vermicelli in the wok, as it has a tendency to spit when added to hot oil.

INGREDIENTS

Serves 4

¹/₂ cup vegetable oil
8 ounces rice vermicelli
5 ounces green beans, trimmed and
   halved lengthwise
1 onion, finely chopped
2 boneless chicken breasts, skinned
   and cut into strips
1 teaspoon chili powder
8 ounces shelled cooked shrimp
3 tablespoons dark soy sauce
3 tablespoons white wine vinegar
2 teaspoons superfine sugar
fresh cilantro sprigs, to garnish

1 Heat a wok, then add ¼ cup of the oil. Break up the vermicelli into 3-inch lengths. When the oil is hot, fry the vermicelli in batches. Remove from the heat, drain and keep warm.

2 Heat the remaining oil in the wok, then add the beans, onion and chicken and stir-fry for 3 minutes, until the chicken is cooked.

3 Sprinkle in the chili powder. Stir in the shrimp, soy sauce, vinegar and sugar, and stir-fry for 2 minutes.

4 Serve the chicken, shrimp and vegetables piled on the fried vermicelli, garnished with sprigs of fresh cilantro.

--- COOK'S TIP ---

There is little consensus about chili powder. Some varieties consist purely of ground, dried, hot chilies, whereas others are a mixture of ground chilies and various other spices and herbs, including oregano and cumin. The latter is more suitable for Mexican cuisine than for use in Asian dishes. In any case, pure ground chili is a more practical choice, as you can include your own additional flavorings if you want to, but you cannot lose any that are already there. Some chili powders even include cheaper "bulking" ingredients, so it is always sensible to read the label carefully before buying. This will also give some indication of how mild or hot the spice is. To be absolutely sure of quality, you can grind your own chili powder from dried chilies in a mortar with a pestle. Wear rubber gloves to protect your hands, and avoid touching your eyes or mouth.

Fried Singapore Noodles

Thai fish cakes add a wonderful spiciness to this stir-fry. Make them yourself or buy them at an Asian supermarket. They vary quite considerably in size and degree of spiciness.

INGREDIENTS

Serves 4

6 ounces rice noodles
¼ cup vegetable oil
½ teaspoon salt
3 ounces shelled cooked shrimp
6 ounces cooked pork, cut into matchsticks
1 green bell pepper, seeded and cut into matchsticks
½ teaspoon sugar
2 teaspoons curry powder
3 ounces Thai fish cakes
2 teaspoons dark soy sauce

1 Soak the rice noodles in water for about 10 minutes, drain well, then pat dry with paper towels.

COOK'S TIP

Rice noodles, called *banh trang*, are made from ground rice and water. They range in thickness from very thin to wide ribbons and sheets. Dried ribbon rice noodles are usually sold tied together in bundles. Fresh rice noodles are also available. Both can be bought at Asian food stores.

2 Heat the wok, then add half the oil. When the oil is hot, add the noodles and half the salt and stir-fry for 2 minutes. Transfer to a heated serving dish and keep warm.

3 Heat the remaining oil and add the shrimp, pork, bell pepper, sugar, curry powder and remaining salt. Stir-fry for 1 minute. Return the noodles to the wok and stir-fry with the fish cakes for 2 minutes. Stir in the soy sauce and serve immediately.

Tomato Noodles with Fried Egg

INGREDIENTS

Serves 4

12 ounces medium-thick
  dried noodles
4 tablespoons vegetable oil
2 garlic cloves, very finely chopped
4 shallots, chopped
½ teaspoon chili powder
1 teaspoon paprika
2 carrots, finely diced
4 ounces button mushrooms,
  quartered
2 ounces peas
1 tablespoon tomato ketchup
2 teaspoons tomato paste
salt and freshly ground black pepper
butter for frying
4 eggs

1 Cook the noodles in a saucepan
of boiling water until just tender.
Drain, rinse under cold running water,
and drain well.

2 Heat the oil in a wok or large
frying pan. Add the garlic, shallots,
chili powder and paprika. Stir-fry for
about 1 minute, then add the carrots,
mushrooms and peas. Continue to
stir-fry until the vegetables are cooked.

3 Stir the tomato ketchup and paste
into the vegetable mixture. Add
the noodles, and cook over a medium
heat until the noodles are heated
through and have taken on the reddish
tinge of the paprika and tomato.

4 Meanwhile, melt the butter in a
frying pan, and fry the eggs. Season
the noodle mixture, divide it among
four serving plates, and top each
portion with a fried egg.

Curry Fried Noodles

On its own, bean curd (tofu) has
a fairly bland flavor, but it takes
on the flavor of the curry spices
wonderfully.

INGREDIENTS

Serves 4

4 tablespoons vegetable oil
2–3 tablespoons curry paste
8 ounces smoked bean curd, cut into
  1-inch cubes
8 ounces green beans, cut into
  1-inch lengths
1 red bell pepper, seeded and cut into
  fine strips
12 ounces rice vermicelli, soaked in
  warm water until soft
1 tablespoon soy sauce
salt and freshly ground black pepper
2 scallions, finely sliced, 2 red chilies,
  seeded and chopped, and 1 lime, cut
  into wedges, to garnish

1 Heat half the oil in a wok or large
frying pan. Add the curry paste,
and stir-fry for a few minutes, then add
the bean curd. Continue to fry until
golden brown. Using a slotted spoon,
remove the cubes from the pan. Set
aside until required.

2 Add the remaining oil to the wok
or pan. When hot, add the green
beans and red pepper. Stir-fry until the
vegetables are cooked. You may need
to moisten them with a little water.

3 Drain the noodles, and add them
to the wok or frying pan. Continue
to stir-fry until the noodles are heated
through, then return the curried bean
curd to the wok. Season with soy
sauce, salt and pepper.

4 Transfer the mixture to a serving
dish. Sprinkle with the scallions
and chilies, and serve the lime wedges
on the side.

Rice Noodles with Beef and Black Bean Sauce

This is an excellent combination – beef with a chili sauce tossed with silky, smooth rice noodles.

INGREDIENTS

Serves 4

1 pound fresh rice noodles
4 tablespoons vegetable oil
1 onion, finely sliced
2 garlic cloves, finely chopped
2 slices fresh ginger, finely chopped
8 ounces mixed bell peppers, seeded and cut into strips
12 ounces round steak, finely sliced against the grain
3 tablespoons fermented black beans, rinsed in warm water, drained and chopped
2 tablespoons soy sauce
2 tablespoons oyster sauce
1 tablespoon chili black bean sauce
1 tablespoon cornstarch
½ cup broth or water
2 scallions, finely chopped, and 2 red chilies, seeded and finely sliced, to garnish

1 Rinse the noodles under hot water. Drain well. Heat half the oil in a wok or large frying pan, swirling it around. Add the onion, garlic, ginger and mixed pepper strips. Stir-fry for 3–5 minutes, then remove with a slotted spoon, and keep hot.

2 Add the remaining oil to the wok. When hot, add the sliced beef and fermented black beans, and stir-fry over a high heat for 5 minutes or until they are cooked.

3 In a small bowl, blend the soy sauce, oyster sauce and chili black bean sauce with the cornstarch and broth or water until smooth. Add the mixture to the wok, then return the onion mixture to the wok and cook, stirring, for 1 minute.

4 Add the noodles, and mix lightly. Stir over a medium heat until the noodles are heated through. Adjust the seasoning, if necessary. Serve at once, garnished with the chopped scallions and chilies.

Buckwheat Noodles with Smoked Trout

The light, crisp texture of the bok choy balances the earthy flavors of the mushrooms, the buckwheat noodles and the smokiness of the trout.

INGREDIENTS

Serves 4

12 ounces buckwheat noodles
2 tablespoons vegetable oil
4 ounces fresh shiitake
  mushrooms, quartered
2 garlic cloves, finely chopped
1 tablespoon grated fresh ginger
8 ounces bok choy
1 scallion, finely sliced diagonally
1 tablespoon dark sesame oil
2 tablespoons mirin
2 tablespoons soy sauce
2 smoked trout, skinned and boned
salt and freshly ground black pepper
2 tablespoons cilantro leaves and
  2 teaspoons sesame seeds, toasted,
  to garnish

1 Cook the buckwheat noodles in a large saucepan of boiling water for about 7–10 minutes or until they are just tender, following the directions on the package.

2 Meanwhile, heat the oil in a large frying pan. Add the shiitake mushrooms, and sauté over a medium heat for 3 minutes. Add the garlic, ginger and bok choy, and continue to sauté for 2 minutes.

3 Drain the noodles, and add them to the mushroom mixture with the scallion, sesame oil, mirin and soy sauce. Toss, and season with salt and pepper to taste.

4 Break the smoked trout in bite-size pieces. Arrange the noodle mixture on individual serving plates. Place the smoked trout on top of the noodles.

5 Garnish the noodles with cilantro leaves and sesame seeds, and serve them immediately.

Tossed Noodles with Seafood

INGREDIENTS

Serves 4–6
12 ounces thick egg noodles
4 tablespoons vegetable oil
3 slices fresh ginger, grated
2 garlic cloves, finely chopped
8 ounces mussels or clams
8 ounces raw shrimp, peeled
8 ounces squid, cut into rings
4 ounces oriental fish cake, sliced
1 red bell pepper, seeded and cut
   into rings
2 ounces sugar snap peas, ends
   removed
2 tablespoons soy sauce
½ teaspoon sugar
½ cup broth or water
1 tablespoon cornstarch
1–2 teaspoons sesame oil
salt and freshly ground black pepper
2 scallions, chopped, and 2 red chilies,
   seeded and chopped, to garnish

1 Cook the noodles in a large saucepan of boiling water until just tender. Drain, rinse under cold water, and drain well.

2 Heat the oil in a wok or large frying pan. Fry the ginger and garlic for 30 seconds. Add the mussels or clams, shrimp and squid, and stir-fry for about 4–5 minutes until the seafood changes color. Add the fish cake slices, bell pepper rings and sugar snap peas, and stir well.

3 In a bowl, mix the soy sauce, sugar, broth or water and cornstarch. Stir into the seafood, and bring to a boil. Add the noodles, and cook until they are heated through.

4 Add the sesame oil to the wok or pan, and season with salt and pepper to taste. Serve at once, garnished with the chopped scallions and red chilies.

Noodles with Spicy Meat Sauce

INGREDIENTS

Serves 4–6
2 tablespoons vegetable oil
2 dried red chilies, chopped
1 teaspoon grated fresh ginger
2 garlic cloves, finely chopped
1 tablespoon chili black bean paste
1 pound minced pork or beef
1 pound broad flat egg noodles
1 tablespoon sesame oil
2 scallions, chopped, to garnish

For the sauce
¼ teaspoon salt
1 teaspoon sugar
1 tablespoon soy sauce
1 teaspoon mushroom ketchup
1 tablespoon cornstarch
1 cup chicken broth
1 teaspoon Shaohsing wine or
   dry sherry

1 Heat the vegetable oil in a large saucepan. Add the dried chilies, ginger and garlic. Fry until the garlic starts to color, then gradually stir in the chili black bean paste.

2 Add the minced pork or beef, breaking it up with a spatula or wooden spoon. Cook over a high heat until the minced meat changes color and any liquid has evaporated.

3 Mix all the sauce ingredients in a cup. Make a well in the center of the pork mixture. Pour in the sauce mixture, and stir together. Simmer for 10–15 minutes until tender.

4 Meanwhile, cook the noodles in a large saucepan of boiling water for 5–7 minutes until just tender. Drain well, and toss with the sesame oil. Serve, topped with the meat sauce and garnished with the scallions.

Noodles with Meatballs

Mie Rebus is a one-pot meal, for which the East is renowned.

INGREDIENTS

Serves 6

1 pound Spicy Meatball mixture
12 ounces dried egg noodles
3 tablespoons sunflower oil
1 large onion, finely sliced
2 garlic cloves, crushed
1 inch fresh ginger root, peeled and cut in thin matchsticks
5 cups broth
2 tablespoons dark soy sauce
2 celery stalks, finely sliced, leaves reserved
6 Chinese cabbage leaves, cut in bite-size pieces
1 handful snow peas, cut in strips
salt and freshly ground black pepper

1 Prepare the meatballs, making them quite small. Set aside.

2 Add the noodles to a large pan of salted, boiling water and stir so that the noodles do not settle at the bottom. Simmer for 3–4 minutes, or until *al dente*. Drain in a colander and rinse with plenty of cold water. Set aside.

3 Heat the oil in a wide pan and fry the onion, garlic and ginger until soft but not browned. Add the broth and soy sauce and bring to a boil.

4 Add the meatballs, half-cover and allow to simmer until they are cooked, about 5–8 minutes depending on size. Just before serving, add the sliced celery and, after 2 minutes, add the Chinese cabbage and snow peas. Taste and adjust the seasoning.

5 Divide the noodles among soup bowls, add the meatballs and vegetables and pour the soup on top. Garnish with the reserved celery leaves.

Stir-fried Rice Noodles with Chicken and Shrimp

Shellfish have a natural affinity with both meat and poultry. This Thai-style recipe combines chicken with shrimp, and has the characteristic sweet, sour and salty flavor.

INGREDIENTS

Serves 4

8 ounces dried flat rice noodles
½ cup water
4 tablespoons fish sauce
1 tablespoon sugar
1 tablespoon fresh lime juice
1 teaspoon paprika
pinch of cayenne pepper
3 tablespoons oil
2 garlic cloves, finely chopped
1 skinless, boneless chicken breast, finely sliced
8 raw shrimp, peeled, deveined and cut in half
1 egg
½ cup roasted peanuts, coarsely crushed
3 scallions, cut into short lengths
6 ounces bean sprouts
cilantro leaves and 1 lime, cut into wedges, to garnish

1 Place the rice noodles in a large bowl, cover with warm water, and soak for 30 minutes until soft. Drain.

2 Combine the water, fish sauce, sugar, lime juice, paprika and cayenne in a small bowl. Set aside until required.

3 Heat the oil in a wok. Add the garlic, and fry for 30 seconds until it starts to brown. Add the chicken and shrimp, and stir-fry for 3–4 minutes until cooked.

4 Push the chicken and shrimp mixture in the wok out to the sides. Break the egg into the center, then quickly stir to break up the yolk. Cook over a medium heat until the egg is just lightly scrambled.

5 Add the drained noodles and the fish sauce mixture to the wok. Mix together well. Add half the crushed peanuts, and cook, stirring frequently, until the noodles are soft and most of the liquid has been absorbed.

6 Add the scallions and half of the bean sprouts. Cook, stirring, for 1 minute more. Spoon onto a platter. Sprinkle with the remaining peanuts and bean sprouts. Garnish with the cilantro and lime wedges, and serve.

Thai Fried Noodles

Phat Thai has a fascinating flavor and texture. It's made with fine rice noodles and is considered one of the national dishes of Thailand.

INGREDIENTS

Serves 4–6

12 ounces rice noodles
3 tablespoons vegetable oil
1 tablespoon chopped garlic
16 uncooked jumbo shrimp, shelled, tails left intact, and deveined
2 eggs, lightly beaten
1 tablespoon dried shrimp, rinsed
2 tablespoons pickled white radish
2 ounces fried tofu, cut into small slivers
½ teaspoon dried chili flakes
4 ounces garlic chives, cut into 2-inch lengths
1 cup bean sprouts
½ cup roasted peanuts, coarsely ground
1 teaspoon sugar
1 tablespoon dark soy sauce
2 tablespoons fish sauce
2 tablespoons tamarind juice
2 tablespoons cilantro leaves and 1 kaffir lime, to garnish

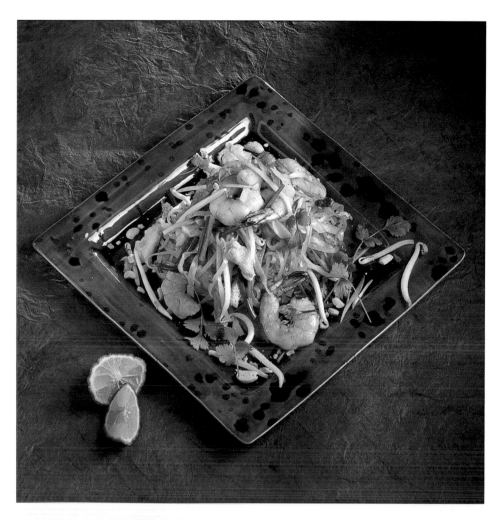

1 Soak the noodles in warm water for 20–30 minutes, then drain.

2 Heat 1 tablespoon of the oil in a wok or large frying pan. Add the garlic and fry until golden. Stir in the shrimp and cook for about 1–2 minutes, until pink, tossing from time to time. Remove and set aside.

3 Heat another 1 tablespoon of oil in the wok. Add the eggs and tilt the wok to spread them into a thin sheet. Stir to scramble and break the eggs into small pieces. Remove from the wok and set aside with the shrimp.

4 Heat the remaining oil in the same wok. Add the dried shrimp, pickled radish, tofu and dried chilies. Stir briefly. Add the soaked noodles and stir-fry for 5 minutes.

5 Add the garlic chives, half the bean sprouts and half the peanuts. Season with the sugar, soy sauce, fish sauce and tamarind juice. Mix together well and cook until the noodles are completely heated through.

6 Return the shrimp and egg mixture to the wok and mix with the noodles. Serve garnished with the rest of the bean sprouts, peanuts, cilantro leaves and lime wedges.

Bamie Goreng

This fried noodle dish is wonderfully accommodating. To the basic recipe you can add other vegetables, such as mushrooms, tiny pieces of chayote, broccoli, leeks or bean sprouts, if you prefer. As with fried rice, you can use whatever you have to hand, bearing in mind the need to achieve a balance of colors, flavors and textures.

INGREDIENTS

Serves 6–8
1 pound dried egg noodle
1 boneless chicken breast, skinned
4 ounces pork loin
4 ounces calf liver (optional)
2 eggs, beaten
6 tablespoons oil
2 tablespoons butter or margarine
2 garlic cloves, crushed
4 ounces cooked shrimp, shelled
4 ounces spinach or Chinese cabbage
2 celery stalks, finely sliced
4 scallions, shredded
about 4 tablespoons chicken broth
dark soy sauce and light soy sauce
salt and ground black pepper
Deep-fried Onions and celery leaves,
  to garnish

1 Cook the noodles in salted, boiling water for 3–4 minutes. Drain, rinse with cold water and drain again. Set aside until required.

2 Finely slice the chicken, pork loin and calf liver, if using.

3 Season the eggs. Heat 1 teaspoon of the oil with the butter or margarine in a small pan until melted and then stir in the eggs and keep stirring until scrambled. Set aside.

4 Heat the remaining oil in a wok and fry the garlic with the chicken, pork and liver, if using, for 2–3 minutes, until they have changed color. Add the shrimp, spinach or Chinese cabbage, celery and scallions, tossing well.

5 Add the cooked and drained noodles and toss again so that all the ingredients are well mixed. Add enough broth just to moisten, and dark and light soy sauce to taste. Finally, stir in the scrambled eggs.

6 Garnish the dish with Deep-fried Onions and celery leaves, and serve immediately.

Somen Noodles with Zucchini

A colorful dish with lots of flavor. Patty pan squashes can be used as an alternative to zucchini.

INGREDIENTS

Serves 4

2 yellow zucchini or summer squash
2 green zucchini
4 tablespoons pine nuts
4 tablespoons extra virgin olive oil
2 shallots, finely chopped
2 garlic cloves, finely chopped
2 tablespoons capers, rinsed
4 sun-dried tomatoes in oil, drained
    and cut into strips
11 ounces somen noodles
4 tablespoons chopped mixed fresh
    herbs (such as chives, lemon thyme,
    and tarragon)
grated rind of 1 lemon
³/₄ cup finely grated Parmesan
    cheese
salt and freshly ground black pepper

1 Slice the zucchini diagonally into rounds the same thickness as the noodles. Cut the zucchini slices into matchsticks. Toast the pine nuts in an ungreased frying pan over a medium heat until golden in color.

2 Heat half the oil in a large frying pan. Add the shallots and garlic, and fry until fragrant. Push the shallot mixture to one side of the pan, add the remaining oil and, when hot, stir-fry the zucchini until soft.

3 Stir thoroughly to incorporate the shallot mixture, and add the capers, sun-dried tomatoes and pine nuts. Remove the pan from the heat.

4 Cook the noodles in a large saucepan of boiling, salted water until just tender, following the directions on the package. Drain well, and toss into the zucchini mixture, adding the herbs, lemon rind and Parmesan, with salt and pepper to taste. Serve at once.

Noodles Primavera

INGREDIENTS

Serves 4

8 ounces dried rice noodles
4 ounces broccoli florets
1 carrot, finely sliced
8 ounces asparagus, cut into
    2-inch lengths
1 red or yellow bell pepper, seeded and
    cut into strips
2 ounces baby corn cobs
2 ounces sugar snap peas,
    ends removed
3 tablespoons olive oil
1 tablespoon chopped fresh ginger
2 garlic cloves, chopped
2 scallions, finely chopped
1 pound tomatoes, chopped
1 bunch arugula leaves
soy sauce, to taste
salt and freshly ground black pepper

1 Soak the noodles in hot water for about 30 minutes until soft. Drain.

2 Blanch the broccoli florets, sliced carrot, asparagus, pepper strips, baby corn and sugar snap peas separately in boiling, salted water. Drain them, rinse under cold water, then drain again. Set aside.

3 Heat the olive oil in a frying pan. Add the ginger, garlic and onions. Stir-fry for 30 seconds, then add the tomatoes, and stir-fry for 2–3 minutes.

4 Add the noodles, and stir-fry for 3 minutes. Toss in the blanched vegetables and arugula leaves. Season with soy sauce, salt and pepper, and cook until the vegetables are tender.

Egg Noodles with Tuna and Tomato Sauce

Raid the pantry, add a few fresh ingredients, and you can produce a scrumptious main meal in a matter of minutes.

INGREDIENTS

Serves 4

3 tablespoons olive oil
2 garlic cloves, finely chopped
2 dried red chilies, seeded
    and chopped
1 large red onion, finely sliced
6 ounces canned tuna, drained
1 cup pitted black olives
14-ounce can plum tomatoes, mashed,
    or 14-ounce can chopped tomatoes
2 tablespoons chopped parsley
12 ounces medium-thick
    egg noodles
salt and freshly ground black pepper

1 Heat the oil in a large frying pan. Add the garlic and chilies, and fry for a few seconds before adding the onion. Fry, stirring, for about 5 minutes until the onion softens.

2 Add the tuna and black olives to the pan, and stir until well mixed. Stir in the tomatoes and any juices. Bring to a boil, season with salt and pepper, add the parsley, then lower the heat and simmer gently.

3 Meanwhile, cook the noodles in boiling water until just tender, following the directions on the package. Drain well, toss the noodles with the sauce, and serve at once.

Stir-fried Noodles with Wild Mushrooms

The greater the variety of wild mushrooms you have available, the more interesting this dish will be. Of course, if you can't find wild mushrooms, then a mixture of cultivated mushrooms can be used instead.

INGREDIENTS

Serves 4

12 ounces broad flat egg noodles
3 tablespoons vegetable oil
4 ounces Canadian or lean bacon, cut
    into small pieces
8 ounces wild mushrooms, trimmed
    and cut in half
4 ounces garlic chives, snipped
8 ounces bean sprouts
1 tablespoon oyster sauce
1 tablespoon soy sauce
salt and freshly ground black pepper

1 Cook the noodles in a large saucepan of boiling water for about 3–4 minutes or until just tender. Drain, rinse under cold water, and drain well.

2 Heat 1 tablespoon of the oil in a wok or large frying pan. Add the bacon, and fry until golden.

3 Using a slotted spoon, transfer the cooked bacon to a small bowl. Set aside until needed.

4 Add the rest of the oil to the wok or pan. When hot, add the mushrooms, and fry for 3 minutes. Add the garlic chives and bean sprouts to the wok. Fry for 3 minutes, then add the drained noodles.

5 Season with salt, pepper, oyster sauce and soy sauce. Continue to stir-fry until the noodles are heated through. Sprinkle the crispy bits of bacon on top, and serve.

Noodles with Sun-dried Tomatoes and Shrimp

INGREDIENTS

Serves 4

12 ounces somen noodles
3 tablespoons olive oil
20 uncooked jumbo shrimp, peeled
  and deveined
2 garlic cloves, finely chopped
3–4 tablespoons sun-dried tomato paste
salt and freshly ground black pepper

For the garnish
handful of basil leaves
2 tablespoons sun-dried tomatoes in
  oil, drained and cut into strips

COOK'S TIP

Pre-made sun-dried tomato paste is often available, however you can make your own simply by processing bottled or canned sun-dried tomatoes with their oil. You could also add a couple of anchovy fillets and some capers, if you like.

1 Cook the noodles in a large saucepan of boiling water until tender, following the directions on the package. Drain.

2 Heat half the oil in a large frying pan. Add the shrimp and garlic, and fry them over a medium heat for 3–5 minutes, until the shrimp turn pink and are firm to the touch.

3 Stir in 1 tablespoon of the sun-dried tomato paste, and mix well. Using a slotted spoon, transfer the shrimp to a bowl, and keep hot.

4 Reheat the oil remaining in the pan. Stir in the rest of the oil with the remaining sun-dried tomato paste. You may need to add a spoonful of water if the mixture is very thick.

5 When the mixture starts to sizzle, toss in the noodles. Add salt and pepper to taste, and mix well.

6 Return the shrimp to the pan, and toss to combine. Serve at once garnished with the basil and strips of sun-dried tomatoes.

Mixed Rice Noodles

A delicious noodle dish made extra special by adding avocado and garnishing with shrimp.

INGREDIENTS

Serves 4

1 tablespoon sunflower oil
1-inch piece fresh ginger, peeled and
  grated
2 garlic cloves, crushed
3 tablespoons dark soy sauce
1 cup green peas, thawed if frozen
1 pound rice noodles
1 pound spinach, stalks removed
2 tablespoons smooth peanut butter
2 tablespoons tahini
⅔ cup milk
1 ripe avocado, peeled and pitted
roasted peanuts and shelled, cooked
  shrimp, to garnish

1 Heat a wok, then add the oil. When the oil is hot, stir-fry the ginger and garlic for 30 seconds. Add 1 tablespoon of the soy sauce and ⅔ cup boiling water.

COOK'S TIP

Do not peel, pit or slice the avocado much in advance of using, as the flesh quickly discolors. Sprinkling with a little lemon or lime juice helps prevent this.

2 Add the peas and noodles, then cook for 3 minutes. Stir in the spinach. Remove the vegetables and noodles, drain and keep warm.

3 Stir the peanut butter, remaining soy sauce, tahini and milk together in the wok, and simmer for 1 minute.

4 Add the vegetables and noodles, slice in the avocado and toss together. Serve piled on individual plates. Spoon some sauce over each portion and garnish with roasted peanuts and shrimp.

Noodles with Asparagus and Saffron Sauce

A rather elegant, summery dish with fragrant saffron cream.

INGREDIENTS

Serves 4

1 pound young asparagus
pinch of saffron threads
1 ounce butter
2 shallots, finely chopped
2 tablespoons white wine
1 cup heavy cream
grated rind and juice of ½ lemon
4 ounces peas
12 ounces somen noodles
½ bunch chervil, coarsely chopped
salt and freshly ground black pepper
grated Parmesan cheese (optional)

1 Cut off the asparagus tips (about 2 inches in length), then slice the remaining spears into short rounds. Steep the saffron in 2 tablespoons boiling water in a cup.

2 Melt the butter in a saucepan, add the shallots, and cook over a low heat for 3 minutes until soft. Add the white wine, cream and saffron infusion. Bring to a boil, reduce the heat, and simmer gently for 5 minutes or until the sauce thickens to a coating consistency. Add the grated lemon rind and juice, with salt and pepper to taste.

3 Bring a large saucepan of lightly salted water to a boil. Blanch the asparagus tips, scoop them out, and add them to the sauce, then cook the peas and short asparagus rounds in the boiling water until just tender. Scoop them out, and add to the sauce.

4 Cook the somen noodles in the same water until just tender, following the directions on the package. Drain, place in a wide pan, and pour the sauce over the top.

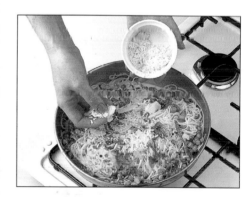

5 Toss the noodles with the sauce and vegetables, adding the chervil and more salt and pepper, if needed. Finally, sprinkle with the grated Parmesan, if using, and serve hot.

Fried Noodles with Bean Sprouts and Asparagus

Soft-fried noodles contrast beautifully with crisp bean sprouts and asparagus.

INGREDIENTS

Serves 4

4 ounces dried egg noodles
¼ cup vegetable oil
1 small onion, chopped
1-inch piece fresh ginger, peeled and grated
2 garlic cloves, crushed
6 ounces young asparagus spears, trimmed
1 cup bean sprouts
4 scallions, sliced
3 tablespoons soy sauce
salt and ground black pepper

1 Bring a pan of salted water to a boil. Add the noodles and cook for 2–3 minutes, until tender. Drain and toss them in 2 tablespoons of the oil.

2 Heat the remaining oil in a preheated wok until very hot. Add the onion, ginger and garlic and stir-fry for 2–3 minutes. Add the asparagus and stir-fry for 2–3 more minutes.

3 Add the noodles and bean sprouts and stir-fry for 2 minutes.

4 Stir in the scallions and soy sauce. Season to taste, adding salt sparingly, as the soy sauce will add quite a salty flavor. Stir-fry for 1 minute, then serve immediately.

Noodles with Ginger and Cilantro

Here is a simple noodle dish that goes well with most Asian dishes. It can also be served as a snack for two or three people.

INGREDIENTS

Serves 4–6
handful of fresh cilantro sprigs
8 ounces dried egg noodles
3 tablespoons peanut oil
2-inch piece fresh ginger, finely shredded
6–8 scallions, shredded
2 tablespoons light soy sauce
salt and ground black pepper

—— COOK'S TIP ——

Many of the dried egg noodles available are sold packed in layers. As a guide, allow 1 layer of noodles per person as an average portion for a main dish.

1 Strip the leaves from the cilantro sprigs. Pile them on a cutting board and chop them roughly, using a cleaver or large, sharp knife.

2 Cook the noodles according to the package instructions. Rinse under cold water and drain well. Toss them in 1 tablespoon of the oil.

3 Heat a wok until hot, add the remaining oil and swirl it around. Add the ginger and stir-fry for a few seconds, then add the noodles and scallions. Stir-fry for 3–4 minutes, until hot.

4 Sprinkle with the soy sauce, cilantro and seasoning. Toss well, then serve immediately.

Stir-fried Tofu and Bean Sprouts with Noodles

This is a satisfying dish, that is both tasty and easy to make.

INGREDIENTS

Serves 4

8-ounce package fresh firm tofu
peanut oil, for deep-frying
6 ounces medium egg noodles
1 tablespoon sesame oil
1 teaspoon cornstarch
2 teaspoons dark soy sauce
2 tablespoons Chinese rice wine or
   dry sherry
1 teaspoon sugar
6–8 scallions, cut diagonally into
   1-inch lengths
3 garlic cloves, sliced
1 fresh green chili, seeded and sliced
1 head bok choy, roughly shredded
½ cup bean sprouts
¼ cup toasted cashews, to garnish

1 Drain the tofu and pat dry with paper towels. Cut the tofu into 1-inch cubes. Half-fill a wok with peanut oil and heat to 350°F. Deep-fry the tofu in batches for 1–2 minutes, until golden and crisp. Drain on paper towels. Carefully pour all but 2 tablespoons of the oil from the wok.

2 Cook the noodles. Rinse them thoroughly under cold water and drain well. Toss them in 2 teaspoons of the sesame oil and set aside. In a bowl, combine the cornstarch, soy sauce, rice wine or sherry, sugar and remaining sesame oil.

3 Reheat the 2 tablespoons of peanut oil and, when hot, add the scallions, garlic, chili, bok choy and bean sprouts. Stir-fry for 1–2 minutes.

4 Add the tofu with the noodles and sauce. Cook, stirring, for about 1 minute, until well mixed. Sprinkle the cashews on top. Serve immediately.

RICE DISHES

Not just one of the world's staples, but one of its favorites too, rice is among the most useful pantry ingredients, providing an easy accompaniment at a few moments' notice or the basis of a main-course dish in hardly any more time. It is the perfect starting point for an amazing range of tastes and flavors combined with a delicious range of other ingredients, herbs and spices. It should not be forgotten that many different types of rice—all with their own distinctive flavors, textures and characteristics—are available to enhance any meal.

Rice with Seeds and Spices

This dish provides a change from plain boiled rice, and is a colorful accompaniment to serve with curries or grilled meats.

INGREDIENTS

Serves 4

1 teaspoon sunflower oil
½ teaspoon ground turmeric
6 green cardamom pods, lightly crushed
1 teaspoon coriander seeds, lightly crushed
1 garlic clove, crushed
1 cup basmati rice
1⅔ cups vegetable stock
½ cup plain yogurt
1 tablespoon toasted sunflower seeds
1 tablespoon toasted sesame seeds
salt and freshly ground black pepper
fresh cilantro leaves, to garnish

1 Heat the oil in a non-stick frying pan and fry the spices and garlic for 1 minute, stirring constantly.

2 Add the rice and stock, bring to a boil, then cover and simmer for 15 minutes or until just tender.

3 Stir in the yogurt and the toasted sunflower and sesame seeds. Adjust the seasoning and serve the rice hot, garnished with cilantro leaves.

Nasi Goreng

One of the most familiar and well-known Indonesian dishes. This is a marvelous way to use up leftover rice, chicken and meats such as pork. It is important that the rice is really cold and the grains separate before adding the other ingredients, so it's best to cook the rice the day before.

INGREDIENTS

Serves 4–6

1⅞ cup long grain rice, such as basmati, cooked and allowed to become completely cold
2 eggs
2 tablespoons water
7 tablespoons oil
8 ounces pork loin or tenderloin of beef
4 ounces cooked, peeled shrimp
6–8 ounces cooked chicken, chopped
2–3 fresh red chilies, seeded and sliced
½ teaspoon shrimp paste
2 garlic cloves, crushed
1 onion, sliced
2 tablespoons dark soy sauce or 3–4 tablespoons tomato ketchup
salt and freshly ground black pepper
celery leaves, Deep-fried Onions and cilantro sprigs, to garnish

1 Once the rice is cooked and cooled, fork it through to separate the grains and keep it in a covered pan or dish until required.

2 Beat the eggs with seasoning and the water and make two or three omelets in a frying pan, with a minimum of oil. Roll up each omelet and cut in strips when cold. Set aside.

3 Cut the pork or beef into neat strips and put the meat, shrimp and chicken pieces in separate bowls. Shred one of the chilies and reserve it.

4 Put the shrimp paste, with the remaining chili, garlic and onion, in a food processor and grind to a fine paste. Alternatively, pound together using a mortar and pestle.

5 Fry the paste in the remaining hot oil, without browning, until it gives off a rich, spicy aroma. Add the pork or beef, tossing the meat constantly, to seal in the juices. Cook for 2 minutes, stirring constantly. Add the shrimp , cook for 2 minutes and then stir in the chicken, cold rice, dark soy sauce or ketchup and seasoning to taste. Stir constantly to prevent the rice from sticking.

6 Turn onto a hot platter and garnish with the omelet strips, celery leaves, onions, reserved shredded chili and the cilantro sprigs.

Thai Fried Rice

This hot and spicy dish is easy to prepare and makes a complete meal in itself.

INGREDIENTS

Serves 4

1½ cups Thai fragrant rice
3 tablespoons vegetable oil
1 onion, chopped
1 small red bell pepper, seeded and cut into ¾-inch squares
2 boneless chicken breasts (12 ounces total), skinned and cubed
1 garlic clove, crushed
1 tablespoon mild curry paste
½ teaspoon paprika
½ teaspoon ground turmeric
2 tablespoons fish sauce
2 eggs, beaten
salt and ground black pepper
fried basil leaves, to garnish

1 Put the rice in a sieve and wash well under cold running water. Put the rice in a heavy pan with 6 cups boiling water. Return to a boil, then simmer, uncovered, for 8–10 minutes; drain well. Spread out the grains on a tray and let cool.

2 Heat a wok until hot, add 2 tablespoons of the oil and swirl it around. Add the onion and red bell pepper and stir-fry for 1 minute.

3 Add the chicken cubes, garlic, curry paste and spices and stir-fry for 2–3 minutes.

4 Reduce the heat to medium, add the cooled rice, fish sauce and seasoning. Stir-fry for 2–3 minutes, until the rice is very hot.

5 Make a well in the center of the rice and add the remaining oil. When hot, add the beaten eggs, let cook for about 2 minutes, until lightly set, then stir into the rice.

6 Scatter the fried basil leaves on top and serve immediately.

COOK'S TIP

Among the various types of rice available, Thai fragrant rice is one of the more popular, especially in Thai, Vietnamese and some other Southeast Asian recipes. It does, in fact, have a particularly special fragrance and is generally served on feast days and other important occasions.

Chinese Jeweled Rice

This rice dish, with its many different, interesting ingredients, is practically a meal in itself.

INGREDIENTS

Serves 4

1½ cups long-grain rice
3 tablespoons vegetable oil
1 onion, roughly chopped
4 ounces cooked ham, diced
6-ounce can white crabmeat
½ cup water chestnuts, drained and cut into cubes
4 dried black Chinese mushrooms, soaked, drained and diced
½ cup green peas, thawed if frozen
2 tablespoons oyster sauce
1 teaspoon sugar
salt

1 Rinse the rice, then cook for 10–12 minutes in 3–3¾ cups salted water in a saucepan with a tight-fitting lid. When cooked, refresh under cold water. Heat half the oil in a preheated wok, then stir-fry the rice for 3 minutes. Remove and set aside.

2 Add the remaining oil to the wok. When the oil is hot, cook the onion until softened but not colored.

3 Add all the remaining ingredients and stir-fry for 2 minutes.

4 Return the rice to the wok and stir fry for 3 minutes, then serve.

Indonesian Fried Rice

This fried rice dish makes an ideal supper on its own or as an accompaniment to another dish.

INGREDIENTS

Serves 4–6

4 shallots, roughly chopped
1 fresh red chili, seeded and chopped
1 garlic clove, chopped
thin sliver of dried shrimp paste
3 tablespoons vegetable oil
8 ounces boneless lean pork, cut into fine strips
1 cup long-grain white rice, cooked and cooled
3–4 scallions, thinly sliced
4 ounces shelled cooked shrimp
2 tablespoons sweet soy sauce
chopped fresh cilantro and fine cucumber shreds, to garnish

1 In a mortar pound the shallots, chili, garlic and shrimp paste with a pestle until they form a paste.

COOK'S TIP

Shrimp paste, sometimes called dried shrimp paste, is a strong-smelling and flavorful paste made from fermented shrimp that is used extensively in many Asian cuisines. Always use sparingly. It is available at most Asian food stores.

---

2 Heat a wok until hot, add 2 tablespoons of the oil and swirl it around. Add the pork and stir-fry for 2–3 minutes. Remove the pork from the wok, set aside and keep warm.

3 Add the remaining oil to the wok. When hot, add the spiced shallot paste and stir-fry for about 30 seconds.

4 Reduce the heat. Add the rice, sliced scallions and shrimp. Stir-fry for 2–3 minutes. Add the pork and sprinkle with the soy sauce. Stir-fry for 1 minute. Serve immediately, garnished with chopped fresh cilantro and cucumber shreds.

Festive Rice

Nasi Kuning is served at special events—weddings, birthdays or farewell parties.

INGREDIENTS

Serves 8

1 pound Thai fragrant rice
4 tablespoons oil
2 garlic cloves, crushed
2 onions, finely sliced
2 inches fresh turmeric, peeled
 and crushed
3 cups water
14-fluid ounce can coconut milk
1–2 lemongrass stalks, bruised
1–2 *pandan* leaves (optional)
salt

For the garnish
omelet strips
2 fresh red chilies, shredded
cucumber chunks
tomato wedges
Deep-fried Onions

1 Wash the rice in several changes of water. Drain well.

2 Heat the oil in a wok and gently fry the crushed garlic, the finely sliced onions and the crushed fresh turmeric for a few minutes until soft but not browned.

COOK'S TIP

It is the custom to shape the rice into a cone (to represent a volcano) and then surround with the garnish ingredients. Shape with oiled hands.

---

3 Add the rice and stir well so that each grain is thoroughly coated. Pour in the water and coconut milk and add the lemongrass, *pandan* leaves, if using, and salt.

4 Bring to a boil, stirring well. Cover and cook gently for about 15–20 minutes, until all of the liquid has been absorbed.

5 Remove from the heat. Cover with a dish towel, put on the lid and let stand in a warm place for 15 minutes. Remove the lemongrass and *pandan* leaves.

6 Turn onto a platter, garnish and serve.

Special Fried Rice

Special Fried Rice is so substantial and tasty that it is another rice dish that is almost a meal in itself.

INGREDIENTS

Serves 4
8 medium cooked shrimp, shelled
1 thick slice cooked ham
½ cup green peas
3 eggs
1 teaspoon salt
2 scallions, finely chopped
¼ cup vegetable oil
1 tablespoon light soy sauce
1 tablespoon Chinese rice wine or
   dry sherry
1 pound cooked rice

1 Pat dry the shrimp with paper towels. Cut the ham into small dice about the same size as the peas.

2 In a bowl, lightly beat the eggs with a pinch of the salt and a few pieces of the scallions.

3 Heat about half of the oil in a preheated wok, stir-fry the peas, shrimp and ham for 1 minute, then add the soy sauce and rice wine or sherry. Remove and keep warm.

4 Heat the remaining oil in the wok and lightly scramble the eggs. Add the rice and stir to make sure that each grain of rice is separated. Add the remaining salt and scallions and the shrimp, ham and peas. Mix well and serve either hot or cold.

Jasmine Rice

A naturally aromatic, long-grain white rice, jasmine rice is the staple of most Thai meals. If you eat rice regularly, you might invest in an electric rice cooker.

INGREDIENTS

Serves 4–6

2 cups jasmine rice
3 cups cold water

COOK'S TIP

An electric rice cooker cooks the rice and keeps it warm. Different sizes and models of rice cookers are available. The top of the range is a nonstick version, which is expensive, but well worth the money.

---

1 Rinse the rice thoroughly, at least three times, in cold water until the water runs clear.

2 Put the rice in a heavy-bottomed saucepan and add the water. Bring the rice to a vigorous boil, uncovered, over high heat.

3 Stir and reduce the heat to low. Cover and simmer for up to 20 minutes, or until all the water has been absorbed. Remove from the heat and allow to stand for 10 minutes.

4 Remove the lid and stir the rice gently with a rice paddle or a pair of wooden chopsticks, to fluff up and separate the grains.

Fried Jasmine Rice with Shrimp and Thai Basil

Thai basil (*bai grapao*), also known as Holy basil, has a unique, pungent flavor that is both spicy and sharp. It can be found in most Asian food markets.

INGREDIENTS

Serves 4–6

3 tablespoons vegetable oil
1 egg, beaten
1 onion, chopped
1 tablespoon chopped garlic
1 tablespoon shrimp paste
4 cups cooked jasmine rice
12 ounces cooked shelled shrimp
⅓ cup thawed frozen peas
oyster sauce, to taste
2 scallions, chopped
15–20 Thai basil leaves, coarsely chopped, plus an extra sprig, to garnish

1 Heat 1 tablespoon of the oil in a wok or frying pan. Add the beaten egg and swirl it around the pan to set like a thin pancake.

2 Cook until golden, slide out on to a board, roll up and cut into thin strips. Set aside.

3 Heat the remaining oil in the wok, add the onion and garlic and fry for 2–3 minutes. Stir in the shrimp paste and mix thoroughly.

4 Add the rice, shrimp and peas and toss together until everything is heated through.

5 Season with oyster sauce to taste, taking great care as the shrimp paste is salty. Add the scallions and basil leaves. Transfer to a serving dish and serve topped with the strips of egg pancake. Garnish with a sprig of basil.

Fried Rice with Pork

If you like, garnish with strips of
omelet, as in Fried Jasmine Rice
with Shrimp and Thai Basil.

INGREDIENTS

Serves 4–6

3 tablespoons vegetable oil
1 onion, chopped
1 tablespoon chopped garlic
4 ounces pork, cut into small cubes
2 eggs, beaten
4 cups cooked rice
2 tablespoons fish sauce
1 tablespoon dark soy sauce
½ teaspoon superfine sugar
4 scallions, finely sliced, to garnish
2 red chilies, sliced, to garnish
1 lime, cut into wedges and egg
   omelet, to garnish (optional)

1 Heat the oil in a wok or large
frying pan. Add the onion and
garlic and cook for about 2 minutes,
until softened.

2 Add the pork to the softened
onion and garlic. Stir-fry until the
pork changes color and is cooked.

3 Add the eggs and cook until
scrambled into small lumps.

4 Add the rice and continue to stir
and toss, to coat it with the oil and
prevent it from sticking.

5 Add the fish sauce, soy sauce and
sugar and mix well. Continue to
fry until the rice is thoroughly heated.
Garnish with sliced scallions, red chilies
and lime wedges. If you like, top with
a few strips of egg omelet.

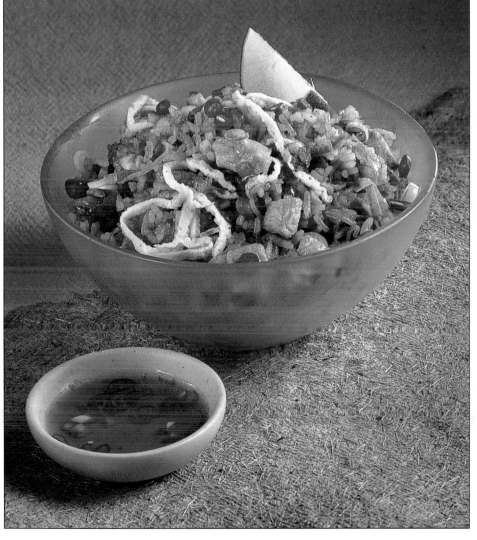

Red Fried Rice

This vibrant rice dish owes its appeal as much to the bright colors of red onion, red bell pepper and cherry tomatoes as it does to their distinctive flavors.

INGREDIENTS

Serves 2
½ cup basmati rice
2 tablespoons peanut oil
1 small red onion, chopped
1 red bell pepper, seeded and chopped
8 ounces cherry tomatoes, halved
2 eggs, beaten
salt and ground black pepper

1 Wash the rice several times under cold running water. Drain well. Bring a large pan of salted water to a boil, add the rice and cook for 10–12 minutes, until tender.

2 Meanwhile, heat the oil in a wok until very hot. Add the onion and bell pepper and stir-fry for 2–3 minutes. Add the cherry tomatoes and stir-fry for another 2 minutes.

3 Pour in the beaten eggs all at once. Cook for 30 seconds without stirring, then stir to break up the egg as it sets.

4 Drain the cooked rice thoroughly, add to the wok and toss it over the heat with the vegetable and egg mixture for 3 minutes. Season the fried rice with salt and pepper to taste.

Spicy Fried Rice Sticks with Shrimp

This well-known recipe is based on the classic Thai noodle dish called *pad Thai*. Popular all over Thailand, it is enjoyed morning, noon and night.

INGREDIENTS

Serves 4

2 tablespoons dried shrimp
1 tablespoon tamarind pulp
3 tablespoons fish sauce
1 tablespoon sugar
2 garlic cloves, chopped
2 fresh red chilies, seeded and chopped
3 tablespoons peanut oil
2 eggs, beaten
8 ounces dried rice sticks, soaked in warm water for 30 minutes, refreshed under cold running water and drained
8 ounces cooked jumbo shrimp, shelled
3 scallions, cut into 1-inch lengths
½ cup bean sprouts
2 tablespoons roughly chopped roasted unsalted peanuts
2 tablespoons chopped fresh cilantro
lime slices, to garnish

1 Put the dried shrimp in a small bowl and pour in enough warm water to cover them. Let soak for 30 minutes, until soft, then drain.

2 Put the tamarind pulp in a bowl with ¼ cup hot water. Blend together, then press through a strainer to extract 2 tablespoons thick tamarind water. Mix the tamarind water with the fish sauce and sugar.

3 Using a mortar and pestle, pound the garlic and chilies to form a paste. Heat a wok over medium heat, add 1 tablespoon of the oil, then add the beaten eggs and stir for 1–2 minutes, until the eggs are scrambled. Remove and set aside. Wipe the wok clean.

COOK'S TIP

For a vegetarian dish, omit the dried shrimp and replace the jumbo shrimp with cubes of deep-fried tofu.

4 Reheat the wok until hot and add the remaining oil, then the chili paste and dried shrimp and stir-fry for 1 minute. Add the rice sticks and tamarind mixture and stir-fry for 3–4 minutes.

5 Add the scrambled eggs, shrimp, scallions, bean sprouts, peanuts and cilantro, then stir-fry for 2 minutes, until well mixed. Serve immediately, garnishing each portion with lime slices.

Fried Rice with Spices

This dish is mildly spiced, and is suitable as an accompaniment to any curried dish. The whole spices—cloves, cardamom, bay leaf, cinnamon, peppercorns and cumin—are not intended to be eaten.

INGREDIENTS

Serves 3–4

¾ cup basmati rice
½ teaspoon salt
1 tablespoon ghee or butter
8 whole cloves
4 green cardamom pods, bruised
1 bay leaf
3-inch piece cinnamon stick
1 teaspoon black peppercorns
1 teaspoon cumin seeds

1 Put the rice in a colander and wash under cold running water until the water runs clear. Put in a bowl and pour 2½ cups fresh water over the rice. Let the rice soak for 30 minutes, then drain thoroughly.

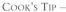

— COOK'S TIP —

You could add ½ teaspoon ground turmeric to the rice in step 2 of the recipe to color it yellow.

2 Put the basmati rice, salt and 2½ cups water in a large, heavy pan. Bring to a boil, then cover and simmer for about 10 minutes. The rice should be just cooked, with a little bite to it. Drain off any excess water, fluff up the grains with a fork, then spread the rice out on a tray and set aside to cool.

3 Heat the ghee or butter in a wok until foaming, add the spices and stir-fry for 1 minute.

4 Add the cooled rice and stir-fry for 3–4 minutes, until warmed through. Serve immediately.

Nutty Rice and Mushroom Stir-fry

This delicious and substantial supper dish can be eaten hot or cold with salads.

INGREDIENTS

Serves 4–6

1½ cups long-grain rice, preferably basmati
3 tablespoons sunflower oil
1 small onion or shallot, roughly chopped
2 cups wild mushrooms, sliced
½ cup hazelnuts, roughly chopped
½ cup pecans, roughly chopped
½ cup almonds, roughly chopped
¼ cup fresh parsley, chopped
salt and ground black pepper

1 Rinse the rice, then cook for 10–12 minutes in 3–3¾ cups salted water in a saucepan with a tight-fitting lid. When cooked, refresh under cold water. Heat a wok, then add half the oil. Stir-fry the rice for 2–3 minutes. Remove and set aside.

COOK'S TIP

Of all the types of long-grain rice, basmati is undoubtedly the king. This long, aromatic grain grows in India, where its name means "fragrant." Basmati rice benefits from being rinsed with plenty of cold water and soaked for 10 minutes before it is cooked.

2 Add the remaining oil and stir-fry the onion or shallot for 2 minutes, until softened but not colored. Mix in the wild mushrooms and stir-fry for 2 minutes.

3 Add all the nuts and stir-fry for 1 minute. Return the rice to the wok and stir-fry for 3 minutes. Season with salt and pepper. Stir in the parsley and serve immediately.

DESSERTS

No meal is truly complete without
something sweet—and preferably
indulgent—at the end. Stir-frying fruit
helps to maintain its color and shape,
so cooking in a wok is an excellent
way to prepare tasty desserts to round
off a meal in style. Other unusual but
easy-to-cook, delicious sweet dishes in
this chapter include mouthwatering
Deep-fried Buñuelos—a kind
of Mexican doughnut—scrumptious
Fried Wontons and Ice Cream and
the gloriously sticky, classic
Chinese Toffee Apples.

Pancakes Filled with Sweet Coconut

Traditionally, the pale green color in the batter for *Dadar Gulung* was obtained from the juice squeezed from *pandan* leaves – a real labor of love. Green food coloring can be used as the modern alternative to this lengthy process.

INGREDIENTS

Makes 12–15 pancakes

¾ cup dark brown sugar
2 cups water
1 *pandan* leaf, stripped through with a fork and tied into a knot
6 ounces dried coconut
oil for frying
salt

For the pancake batter

8 ounces flour, sifted
2 eggs, beaten
2 drops edible green food coloring
few drops vanilla extract
scant 2 cups water
3 tablespoons peanut oil

1 Dissolve the sugar in the water with the *pandan* leaf, in a pan over gentle heat, stirring constantly. Increase the heat and allow to boil gently for 3–4 minutes, until the mixture just becomes syrupy. Do not let it caramelize.

2 Put the coconut into a wok with a pinch of salt. Pour over the prepared sugar syrup and cook over a very gentle heat, stirring from time to time, until the mixture becomes almost dry; this will take 5–10 minutes. Set aside until required.

3 To make the batter, blend together the flour, eggs, food coloring, vanilla extract, water and oil either by hand or in a food processor.

4 Brush a 7-inch frying pan with oil and cook 12–15 pancakes. Keep the pancakes warm. Fill each pancake with a generous spoonful of the coconut mixture, roll up and serve them immediately.

Classic Noodle Pudding

A traditional Jewish recipe, Classic Noodle Pudding is a rich and comforting dessert. It is also quite delicious.

INGREDIENTS

Serves 4–6

6 ounces wide egg noodles
1 cup cottage cheese
½ cup cream cheese
½ cup superfine sugar
2 eggs
½ cup sour cream
1 teaspoon vanilla extract
pinch of ground cinnamon
pinch of grated nutmeg
½ teaspoon grated lemon rind
4 tablespoons butter
¼ cup slivered almonds
½ cup fine dried white bread crumbs
confectioner's sugar for dusting

1 Preheat the oven to 350°F. Grease a shallow baking dish. Cook the noodles in a large saucepan of boiling water until just tender. Drain well.

2 Beat the cottage cheese, cream cheese and sugar together in a bowl. Add the eggs, one at a time, and stir in the sour cream. Stir in the vanilla extract, ground cinnamon, grated nutmeg and lemon rind.

3 Fold the noodles into the cheese mixture. Spoon into the prepared baking dish, and level the surface.

4 Melt the butter in a frying pan. Add the almonds, and fry for about 1 minute. Remove from the heat.

5 Stir in the bread crumbs, mixing well. Sprinkle the mixture over the pudding. Bake for 30–40 minutes or until the mixture is set. Serve hot, dusted with a little confectioner's sugar.

Mango and Coconut Stir-fry

Choose a ripe mango for this recipe. If you buy one that is a little underripe, let it sit in a warm place for a day or two before using.

INGREDIENTS

Serves 4
¼ coconut
1 large ripe mango
juice and finely grated zest of 2 limes
1 tablespoon sunflower oil
1 tablespoon butter
2 tablespoons honey
crème fraîche, to serve

1 Prepare the coconut flakes by draining the milk from the coconut and peeling the flesh with a vegetable peeler.

2 Peel the mango. Cut the pit out of the middle of the fruit. Cut each half of the mango into slices.

3 Place the mango slices in a bowl and pour the lime juice and zest over them, to marinate.

4 Meanwhile heat a wok, then add 2 teaspoons of the oil. When the oil is hot, add the butter. When the butter has melted, stir in the coconut flakes and stir-fry for 1–2 minutes, until the coconut is golden brown. Remove and drain on paper towels. Wipe out the wok. Strain the mango slices, reserving the juice.

5 Heat the wok and add the remaining oil. When the oil is hot, add the mango and stir-fry for 1–2 minutes, then add the juice and let bubble and reduce for 1 minute. Stir in the honey, sprinkle the coconut flakes on top and serve with crème fraîche.

COOK'S TIP

You can sometimes buy "fresh" coconut that has already been cracked open and is sold in pieces ready for use at supermarkets, but buying the whole nut ensures greater freshness. Choose one that is heavy for its size and shake it so that you can hear the milk sloshing around. A "dry" coconut will almost certainly have rancid flesh. You can simply crack the shell with a hammer, preferably with the nut inside a plastic bag, but it may be better to pierce the two ends with a sharp nail or skewer first in order to collect and save the coconut milk. An alternative method is to drain the milk first and then heat the nut briefly in the oven until it cracks. Whichever method you choose, it is then fairly easy to extract the flesh and chop or shave it.

Fried Bananas

These delicious treats are a favorite among children and adults alike. They are sold as snacks all day and night at portable roadside stalls and market places throughout Thailand. This recipe works just as well with other fruits, such as pineapple and apple.

INGREDIENTS

Serves 4

1 cup all-purpose flour
½ teaspoon baking soda
2 tablespoons sugar
1 egg
6 tablespoons water
2 tablespoons shredded coconut or
   1 tablespoon sesame seeds
4 firm bananas
oil, for deep-frying
salt
mint sprigs and lychees, to decorate
2 tablespoons honey, to serve

1 Sift the flour, baking soda and a pinch of salt into a bowl. Stir in the sugar. Whisk in the egg and just enough water to make a thin batter. Whisk in the shredded coconut or the sesame seeds.

2 Peel the bananas. Carefully cut each one in half lengthwise, then cut in half horizontally.

3 Heat the oil in a preheated wok. Dip the bananas in the batter, then gently drop a few pieces at a time into the hot oil. Fry until golden brown.

4 Remove the bananas from the oil and drain on paper towels. Serve immediately with honey, if using, and decorate with mint sprigs and lychees.

COOK'S TIP

Buy bananas that are just approaching ripeness and are mostly yellow but still green at the tips, so that they hold their shape and do not disintegrate during cooking. Completely ripe bananas—with yellow, speckled skins—are likely to fall apart, but will be very sweet.

Buñuelos

INGREDIENTS

Serves 6

2 cups all-purpose flour
1 teaspoon baking powder
½ teaspoon salt
1 tablespoon granulated sugar
1 large egg, beaten
½ cup milk
2 tablespoons unsalted butter,
  melted
oil, for frying
granulated sugar, for dusting

For the syrup
1⅓ cups light brown sugar
3 cups water
1 inch cinnamon stick
1 clove

1 Make the syrup. Combine all the ingredients in a saucepan. Heat, stirring, until the sugar has dissolved, then simmer until the mixture is reduced to a light syrup. Remove and discard the spices. Keep the syrup warm while you make the *buñuelos*.

2 Sift the flour, baking powder and salt into a bowl. Stir in the sugar. In a mixing bowl, whisk the egg and the milk well together. Gradually stir in the dry mixture, then beat in the melted butter to make a soft dough.

3 Turn the dough onto a lightly floured board and knead until it is smooth and elastic. Divide the dough into 18 even-size pieces. Shape into balls. With your hands, flatten the balls to disks about 2 inches thick.

4 Use the floured handle of a wooden spoon to poke a hole through the center of each *buñuelo*. Pour oil into a deep frying pan to a depth of 2 inches. Alternatively, use a deep-fryer. Heat the oil to 375°F, or until a cube of day-old bread added to the oil browns in 30–60 seconds.

5 Fry the fritters in batches, taking care not to overcrowd the pan, until they are puffy and golden brown on both sides. Lift out with a slotted spoon and drain on paper towels.

6 Dust the *buñuelos* with sugar and serve with the syrup.

COOK'S TIP

Make the syrup ahead of time if you prefer, and chill it until ready to use, when it can be warmed through quickly.

Sopaipillas

INGREDIENTS

Makes about 30

2 cups all-purpose flour, sifted
1 tablespoon baking powder
1 teaspoon salt
2 tablespoons shortening or margarine
³/₄ cup water
corn oil, for deep-frying
syrup or honey, to serve

COOK'S TIP

Use your imagination when deciding what to serve with the puffs. Sprinkle them with cinnamon and sugar, or syrup flavored with rum. The fat little pillows could even be served plain, as they taste delicious.

---

1 Put the flour, baking powder and salt in a large bowl. Lightly rub in the shortening or margarine, using your fingertips, until the mixture resembles coarse bread crumbs.

2 Gradually stir in the water, using a fork, until the mixture clumps together to form a soft dough.

3 Shape the dough into a ball, then turn out onto a lightly floured surface and knead very gently until smooth. Roll out thinly to a rectangle measuring about 15 x 18 inches. Using a sharp knife, carefully cut into about 30 3-inch squares. For a decorative edge, you could use a pastry wheel to cut out the squares.

4 Heat the oil to 375°F or until a cube of day-old bread browns in 30–60 seconds.

5 Fry the puffs, a few at a time, in the oil. As they puff up, turn over to cook the other side. Remove with a slotted spoon and drain on paper towels. Serve warm, with syrup, honey or any sauce of your choice.

Toffee Apples

A variety of fruits, such as bananas and pineapple, can be prepared and cooked in this way.

INGREDIENTS

Serves 4
4 firm apples
1 cup all-purpose flour
about ¹/₂ cup water
1 egg, beaten
vegetable oil, for deep-frying, plus
    2 tablespoons for the toffee
³/₄ cup sugar

1 Peel and core each apple and cut into eight pieces. Dust each piece of apple with a little of the flour.

2 Sift the remaining flour into a mixing bowl, then slowly add the cold water and stir well to make a smooth batter. Add the beaten egg and blend well.

3 Heat the oil for deep-frying in a wok. Dip the apple pieces in the batter and deep-fry for about 3 minutes, or until golden. Remove and drain. Drain off the oil.

4 Heat the remaining oil in the wok, add the sugar and stir constantly until the sugar has caramelized. Quickly add the apple pieces and blend well so that each piece of apple is thoroughly coated with the toffee. Dip the apple pieces in cold water to harden before serving.

Wonton Twists

These little twists are perfect when you want a quick snack.

INGREDIENTS

Makes 24
12 wonton wrappers
1 egg, beaten
1 tablespoon black sesame seeds
oil for deep-frying
confectioner's sugar for
  dusting (optional)

1 Cut the wonton wrappers in half. Make a lengthwise slit in the center of each piece with a sharp knife.

2 Take one wonton at a time, and pull one end through the slit, stretching it a little as you go.

3 Brush each twist with a little beaten egg. Dip the wonton twists briefly in black sesame seeds to coat them lightly.

4 Heat the oil in a deep-fryer or large saucepan to 375°F. Add a few wonton twists at a time so they do not overcrowd the pan. Fry the twists for 1–2 minutes on each side until crisp and light golden brown. Remove each twist, and drain on paper towels. Dust with confectioner's sugar, if you like, and serve at once.

> — COOK'S TIP —
>
> Use ordinary sesame seeds in place of the black ones, if you prefer.

Fried Wontons and Ice Cream

Here is the Chinese equivalent of American cookies and ice cream. Serve it with fresh or poached fruits or fruit sauces for an impressive treat.

INGREDIENTS

Serves 4
oil for deep-frying
12 wonton wrappers
8 scoops of your favorite ice cream

> — COOK'S TIP —
>
> Try using two flavors of ice cream – chocolate and strawberry perhaps, or vanilla and coffee. For a sophisticated adults-only treat, drizzle over a spoonful of your favorite liqueur.

1 Heat the oil in a deep-fryer or large saucepan to 375°F.

3 Let the cooked wontons drain on paper towels.

2 Add a few wonton wrappers at a time so that they do not crowd the pan too much. Fry for 1–2 minutes on each side until the wrappers are crisp and light golden brown.

4 To serve, place one wonton on each plate. Place a scoop of ice cream on top of each wonton. Top with a second wonton, then add another scoop of ice cream, and finish with a final wonton. Serve at once.

Index